Rhymes of Rajputana

Col. G H Trevor

Low Price Publications
Delhi-110052

Distributed By
D K Publishers Distributors P Ltd.
24, Ansari Road, Darya Ganj,
New Delhi-110002
Phones: 3278368, 3261465, 3278584, 3201514
Fax : 3264368
visit us at: www.dkpd.com
e-mail: dkpd@del3.vsnl.net.in

First Published 1894

Reprinted in LPP 2002

ISBN 81-7536-293-6

Published By
Low Price Publications
A-6, Nimri Commercial Centre,
Near Ashok Vihar Phase-IV,
Delhi-110052
Phone: 7401672, 7452453
visit us at: www.lppindia.com
e-mail: lpp@nde.vsnl.net.in

Printed At
D K Fine Art Press P Ltd.
Delhi-110052

PRINTED IN INDIA

RHYMES OF RAJPUTANA

BY

COL. G. H. TREVOR, C.S.I.
AGENT TO THE GOVERNOR-GENERAL FOR RAJPUTANA

London
MACMILLAN AND CO.
AND NEW YORK
1894

RHYMES OF RAJPUTANA

BY

COL. G. H. TREVOR, C.S.I.

AGENT TO THE GOVERNOR-GENERAL FOR RAJPUTANA

London

MACMILLAN AND CO.

AND NEW YORK

1894

PREFACE

In 1829 Colonel James Tod, after an intimate personal acquaintance with the Rajput States dating from 1806 to 1822, published in two big volumes his famous work entitled *The Annals and Antiquities of Rajasthan*, which is still the chief authority recognised by natives of the country as well as Europeans in all that pertains to the Rajasthan of former days. In that book he laid open from almost every known source, including the classics of Hindustan, local bards and tradition, a mine of information and romance regarding his beloved Rajputs, whom he identified as connected with "the Getic nations described by Herodotus" and the Scandinavian Asi and German tribes. "The heroes of Odin," he writes, "never relished a cup of mead more than the Rajpoot his *madhva*, and the bards of Scandinavia and Rajwarra are alike eloquent in the praise of the bowl." Again: "Even in the heaven of Indra, the Hindoo warrior's paradise, akin to Valhalla, the Rajpoot has his cup which is served by the Apsara, the twin sister of the celestial Hebe of Scania." "Rajasthan," he explains, "is the collective and classical denomination of that portion of India which is the abode of (Rajpoot) princes. In the familiar dialect of these countries it is termed *Rajwarra*, but by the more refined Raet'hana, corrupted to Rajpootana, the common designation among the British to denote the Rajpoot principalities."

The Jat States of Bhurtpore and Dholpore and the Mahomedan State of Tonk have also been included for many years in Rajputana.

Most of the Rhymes in these pages refer to history more or less ancient, and the ground-work of these may be found in Tod's book. For the story of two I am indebted to Powlett's *Gazetteer of Bikanir.* A few of modern cast are added by way of contrast under the head *Miscellaneous.* Should they collectively lead any English reader to take an interest in Rajasthan past and present, my object in publishing them, as a farewell tribute of friendship to the Chiefs and people of that delightful country from whom I have received much kindness, will have been accomplished.

I trust the Notes at the end will not seem too long: they are mainly extracts from Tod, and the uninitiated would do well to glance at them before reading the Rhymes they explain or illustrate. It will be seen that in some Rhymes I have imagined a local guide or bard speaking to an English traveller, in a way which to those who know the country and how difficult it is to extract any information or sentiment from such persons, generally conspicuous by their absence, will seem indeed an effort of imagination. It is an old device, however, and may plead the sanction of usage and Sir Walter Scott.

Lastly, must I ask scientific orthography to pardon colloquialisms like Oodeypore, Jeypore, Jodhpore, instead of Udaipur, Jaipur, Jodhpur, for the sake of rhyme, if for nothing else? I have followed the modern method only in spelling words which I thought would not be familiar to the English reader. Thus, though I cannot dethrone *Suttee* and *nuzzer* in favour of *Sati* and *nazar*, I write Amra and Jagat where Tod wrote Umra and Juggut; herein following, with a halting step, a rule now generally accepted in English newspapers and railway time-tables published in this country as well as by the Government of India for official correspondence.

The Rhymes entitled "Stepping the Boundary," "A

Petition," "Snake-Bite," "A Thakur at Home" have appeared before in a little volume called *Whiffs* published by Messrs. Wheeler and Co., Calcutta and Allahabad (Indian Railway Library Series), the copyright of which belongs to me.

MOUNT ABU, *September* 1894.

CONTENTS

MOUNT ÁBU

OLYMPUS is this hill, from ages
Unknown it has been sacred ground ;
Rishis and Múnis,[1] gods and sages
Dwelt in these woods and rocks around.

And now perchance when earthquake rumbling
Goes muttering thro' the mountain-side,
It may be some old god a-grumbling
At want of worship, wounded pride.

Yet superstition, which by horror
   And promise long has reigned supreme,
Brings thousands yearly to Dilwarra,
   Whose temples surely are a dream :

A dream beyond all comprehension
   Of art that e'en a Goth might saint ;
No wonder if they draw attention
   To lore and legend growing faint.

The worship of the Jain who raised them
   Has now diminished thro' the land,
But pilgrims who have come and praised them
   Are not required to understand.

The white man smiles and from a guide-book chatters
  Of Vishnu, Parasnáth, of Brahman, Jain;
The brown one looks on worship, faith, as matters
  Ordained for each race by a different sign.

Whether he climb to trace in cave or high nook
  The footsteps of some deity, or kneel
Before Dilwarra's gods or those of Gae Mukh,
  Enough for him, unlettered soul, to feel,

Whoe'er in Abuji[2] may rule as master,
  Men of an ancient creed or men without
The *pooja*[3] of his childhood and his pastor
  Is his to follow, let who may have doubt.

He hears unmoved how the Chauhan once wrested
From the Pramar this mountain hold sublime;
His thoughts are further back, when Vishnu crested
Proud Guru Sikr [4] in the world's young prime.

So the old stream of pilgrims ripples yearly,
While some there be who stay awhile and grow
To love the Hill and its cool breezes dearly,
As refuge from the burning plains below:

As clothed with natural, not celestial beauty—
A home for children of the Frank, and place
For England's soldiers when on foreign duty
Health to renew and tired nerve to brace.

To these the rocks which bear the names of *Nun*
And *Toad*, *The Gates* and *Sunset Point*, the play
Of light upon the Lake from Moon and Sun
Are Abu's chief divinities to-day.

[1] The *Rishis* were the great sages; seven are especially enumerated in the Puranas, among whom Viswamitra and Vasishta are frequently mentioned in the legendary lore of Abu.

Múni is a similar term, meaning any great sage or holy man.

[2] The suffix *ji* denotes respect, honour. Natives generally speak of Abu as Abu*ji*, and chiefs and others of less degree have always this suffix attached to their names when mentioned by their own countrymen.

[3] Worship.

[4] Guru Sikr, or the Guru's Pinnacle, is the loftiest peak of Abu, and about ten miles from the civil station. The shrine there has no architectural beauty. The principal objects of worship are contained in a cavern, and consist of a rock of granite bearing the impress of the feet of Data Brija, an incarnation of Vishnu; and in another corner of the cavern are the "puddaca," or footsteps of Rama Nanda, the great apostle of the Sita ascetics. There are also other caves on Guru Sikr resorted to by the numerous pilgrims to this noted shrine. —*Rajputana Gazetteer*.

AJMERE.[1]

SEVENTEEN centuries and a half, they say,
Have passed since Ája the Chauhan this town
And fortress founded: many a stormy day
Since then has Ajmere known: on his way down
To Somnáth Mahmud Sultán made an end,
Nearly nine hundred years ago, of all
That Táragarh was helpless to defend.
Then he who built the tank which people call
The Bisal ságar and who Delhi took
Ruled here awhile: his grandson Ána made
The lake on which the Moghal loved to look
When Shah Jahan long after marble laid

Upon its bank. From Ána sprang the last
  Chauhan who reigned at Delhi ; his great name
Of Prithi Raj still shines throughout the past,
  The topmost pinnacle of Rajput fame.

Since then what changes in seven hundred years—
  Since Saiyad Husein, Moslem governor
Of Táragarh, of whom the traveller hears
  At his famed shrine, surprised by the Rahtore,
Yielded his life and trust!
When England bled,
  Ere the third Richard gained his bloody throne,
For York and Lancaster, White Rose and Red,
  Méwar was Ajmere's lord. It came to own
Lordship from Malwa after, once again
  Islám. The Rahtore for a space held sway,
Till mighty Akbar heralded long reign

Of Moghal, who had ruled perchance to-day
Had Aurangzeb been like him. The last century
Saw Toork,[2] Rahtore, Mahratta, each in turn
Snatching and keeping, till "by Heaven's decree"
The year which made the British bonfires burn
For Waterloo brought Ajmere peace and hope,
Safe in old England's arms.
Here, Father Time,
Let me look back thro' thy kaleidoscope
Of war and slaughter, chivalry and crime,
Upon this scene of hill, and lake, and town
Nestling in lap of Táragarh, most fair,
And linger from its memories of renown
On four great pictures wondrous to compare.

[1] This is the common spelling, which I have followed also in rhyming to Jesalmere, Bikanir, etc., though strictly speaking it would be correct to write and pronounce Ajmér, Jesalmér, Bikanér.

[2] The Rajputs and others apply this word generally to all Mahomedans.

I

AKBAR'S VOW

AKBAR the King was sad and craved a son,
And vowed a vow that if his prayer bore fruit
He thanks to render God would walk on foot
To Ajmere's famous shrine. The gift was won,
The vow fulfilled. Each day the march begun
With all the Eastern pomp of drum and flute,
Horses and elephants and guns' salute.
Three hundred years since then their race have run
And the old shrine hath many a pilgrim seen,
But never since that long procession glowed
And flashed and hummed and trumpeted hath been
A sight like that along the Jeypore road,
Still marked by Akbar's milestones. Nor, I ween,
Hath saint to greater pilgrim favour showed.

II

SIR THOMAS ROE AT AJMERE

A.D. 1616-1618

WHEN James the First of old sent embassy
To Ind, Great Britain's first ambassador
Sought audience of the Moghal emperor
Here at Ajmere, and in his Diary
Tells, in old English, how he patiently
" Laye " a full year, angling with goodly store
Of gifts and compliment, while waiting for
The firmán which, thro' humble factory
And leave to trade, unconscious paved the way
To Clive and Warren Hastings. Who could know,
As by this lake Jahangir proudly lay,
Pavilioned with Eastern pomp and show,
The danger to the Peacock Throne that day
He gave the firmán to Sir Thomas Roe?

III

DIXON SAHIB A.D. 1837-57

The name of Colonel Dixon, who ruled over Merwara from A.D. 1836 to 1857, and over Ajmere also for most of that period, is a household word in both districts, and his tomb at Beawur is still an object of veneration and pilgrimage.

THE land he governed was almost unknown
To the great world outside it when he came;
And when he died, tho' thousands there made moan,
England at least had never heard his name.

For twenty years untrammelled by routine,
Scarcely a white face near him, with rare art
Tanks, villages, he made: and reigned serene
Till the great Mutiny. That broke his heart.

For honour he had neither badge nor star,
But marked an epoch: people still describe
His deeds with love and wonder; near and far
They speak and date from time of "Dixon Sahib."

IV

THE MAYO COLLEGE[1]

A.D. 1890

THE history of Rajwarra reeks with war ;
  But since there came the long, long reign of peace
And ordered law is growing governor,
  With fruits of knowledge yielding rich increase,
A dream was born—to bring the land's chief flower
  Of Youth to love the bloom of gracious arts
That have, or ought to have, a greater power
  Than swords to force a fellowship of hearts.
So this white hall of marble, this green park,
  And these fair houses where glad school-boys dwell

And play arose—a light from out the dark.
Ah, noble dream, the buds begin to swell.
May summer crown thy spring, and autumn bright
Thy message long proclaim "Let there be light." [2]

[1] Founded at Ajmere in 1875 by the Earl of Mayo, Viceroy and Governor-General of India, for the education of the chiefs and nobility of Rajputana.

[2] This is the motto of the College.

AT BHINAI

MADLIA BHEEL [1]

TWO hundred feet above the plain
Upon this rock he made his nest,
And scoured the country round : in vain
The wheeling squadron's frequent quest.
Nor horse nor man, nor lead nor steel,
Could hurt a hair of Madlia Bheel.

That was three hundred years ago.
  This hill and those on either side
And all around them, you must know,
  Were jungle; thick enough to hide
A legion: so the Bheel abode
In safety, ravaging the road.

The King had armies in the south,
  So convoys passed; and more than one
Was looted near that gorge's mouth:
  Till news of what the Bheel had done
And how his name inspired fear
Reached Delhi and the Emperor's ear.

My ancestor brave Karam Sén
  Was with the King at Delhi then,
A Jodhpore prince. He took a train,
  It might be of some hundred men,
And hither came and camped a mile
From this, and planned a stroke of wile.

Five seeming robbers herding kine
  Strayed to the jungle's edge one night,
And sate them down to feast, with wine
  The taste of which was rare delight:
When of a sudden on their meal
Broke in the outlaw Madlia Bheel.

They hailed him for their hearts' own lord,
    Pointed toward the kine and laughed
A welcome to their feast: they poured
    Down every throat the luscious draught—
Wine such as Bheel could never know.
It lured them to their overthrow.

For Karam Sén sharp swordsmen had
    In ambush. In his drunken sleep
He killed the Bheel. The King was glad,
    And gave him all these lands to keep—
Almost as far as sees the eye,
And made him Raja of Bhinai.

The blood of Jodhpore in my veins
  From Karam Sén of princely line,
No village of his broad domains
  Should now own other rule than mine.
But many a one has passed away:
Alas, not half remain to-day.

Lord of the Eighty-four,[2] the name
  My fathers bore for many a year
Was never mine: not mine the blame.
  Ah, well! you do not care to hear
That story now; you only feel
An interest in Madlia Bheel.

This eagle's nest, this rugged peak
  Where once he lived is now my fort.
Here in the Rains I've spent a week,
  But now my breath is getting short
For climbing, and the hill is mute,
Save only for a chance salute

From yonder gun. The kite and crow
  Muse o'er the fortunes of the place.
Bhinai there peacefully below
  Lies with a smile upon her face,
Her tanks and fields, without a thought
Of days when Madlia reived and fought.

Thus he the Raja, bright with sheen
Of pearls and silks of richest hue,
And all a peacock's pride of mien:
I gazed upon the wide-spread view,
And wished that fairer stroke of steel
Had robbed the nest of Madlia Bheel.

[1] This is little more than a translation in verse of the story of Madlia told me by Raja Mangal Singh, C.I.E., of Bhinai, while we were standing together on the top of Madlia's Hill. Alas that my good friend, a most picturesque specimen of a Rajput nobleman of the old type, who was constantly dwelling on the decadence of his dignity and possessions as compared with bygone days, died four years afterwards in 1892.

[2] The *chaurăsi*, or eighty-four (villages), was the old designation of the Raja's domain. Tod writes: "The country was partitioned into districts, each containing from fifty to a hundred towns and villages, though sometimes exceeding that proportion. The great number of *chaurăsis* leads to the conclusion that portions to the amount of eighty-four had been the general subdivision. Many of these yet remain . . . tantamount to the old hundreds of our Saxon ancestry."—Tod, vol. i. p. 141.

AT OODEYPORE

On the Pichola Lake

A local guide is supposed to be addressing an Englishman who is in a boat fishing.

Rama and Krishna both from Manu came
  (You call him Noah but in our Purans
His name is *Vaivaswáta*, the Sun-born)
Thousands of years before your prophet Christ.
The Solar Race from Rama, ancestor
To Méwar, Marwar, Jeypore, Bikanir;
The Lunar, Krishna-born, holds Jesalmere,
Bhatti, Jaréja, and some other tribes.

That is the answer to your question why
    Upon the ceiling of the Mayo College
    Where our young Thákurs go to pick up knowledge
The Sun and Moon blaze out in heraldry.
A golden sun upon a crimson field
Is Méwar's banner; and a frequent sign
The Peacock everywhere, our bird divine.
Our tribes and customs all have been revealed
By Tod Sahib—was there ever such a man?
You know we are Sesodia,[1] that the scribes
Make us the first of six-and-thirty tribes,
And that we are the only Rajput clan
Who never gave a princess to the line
Of Timoor; against which we held our own—
Save at Chitor, our capital of old,
Of which a separate story shall be told—
Since Bappa Rawal founded there his throne

And the old dynasty surnamed Gehlote.
Tod makes our Bappa A.D. 728,[2]
And Oodeypore[3] from Oodey Singh to date,
More than eight centuries later—Akbar's time.
Our history is full of deeds sublime,
Our land of hills and forests—yes, and lakes
Most beautiful to see: the traveller makes
Pictures of this on which we are afloat
('Tis named Pichola), and the Lord Sahib said
(Lord Lansdowne fished, Sir, from this very boat)
He never saw a more enchanting scene:
The Duke[4] too said so—son, Sir, of the Queen.

That's the Maharana's palace. Yes, his rank
Is very high; the biggest state may thank
Its fortune when it weds with Oodeypore.
Our barons too are men of high degree—

Thákurs [5] we call them—tho' sometimes you see
Thákurs in other parts who are no more
Than petty squires: they have a theory,
Maintained for many a century, that while
The Chief and they are one large family,
He service to receive is lord and king,
First of the brotherhood in everything,
But cannot set aside by force or guile
Rights in the land which their forefathers held.
The Durbars (that's the chiefs) have frequently
Troubles with Thákurs, which, at one time quelled
By arms, the British Government
Now settles: often they are caused or swelled
By Brahmans whispering softly in the ear
Of both when angry, fostering discontent
For private purposes. Their influence here
Is strong; they are a race we all revere.

For did not Manu say a Brahman's life
Was worth four soldiers', eight of trading men,
And sixteen Sudras'?[6] That is why since then
Meddling with Chief or Thákur or Dewan
They always manage to put by a bit,
And are so clever in creating strife
For other people, keeping out of it
Themselves, like lawyers feeding on
The quarrels of their clients.
If you wish
To see the city, the Victoria Hall
And Lansdowne Hospital, I'll show you all
The local sights—Bravo! you've hooked a fish.

[1] The clan takes its name from the town Sesodia in Méwar.

[2] See Note, p. 206.

[3] "Classically Udyapoora, the City of the East, from Udya, the point of sunrise."

[4] His Royal Highness the Duke of Connaught visited Oodeypore in 1889, and the Marquess of Lansdowne as Viceroy in 1890.

[5] The first syllable of this word should be pronounced as in the German *thaler*.

[6] As observed by Tod, the following is the climax of Manu's texts protecting the Brahman :—

"What prince could gain wealth by oppressing these (Brahmans), who, if angry, could frame other worlds, and regents of worlds, and could give birth to new gods and mortals?" See Note, p. 207.

AT CHITOR

I

A local bard is supposed to be speaking to an English traveller.

YOU have heard the story before—
Padmani [1] the peerless, the fair,
Who came from the cinnamon shore
Of Ceylon, the Lunkah of yore,
And how in Méwar we swear
"By the sin of the sack of Chitor"?
Three sacks and a half we count.
Of the half I will tell you first :

A tale of a traitor accurst
And of beauty ill-fated, the fount
Of a chivalry such as the Turk
Never showed in the days that have been,
And of slaughter—alas for that scene !—
God's curse upon Allah-ud-din,
His race and their handiwork !

Her beauty all the world inspired,
Till he, the King, by passion fired,
Resolved to lead an army here
And take by craft, or sword and spear,
A robber's might, that peerless girl,
Brave Bheemsi's [2] queen and Méwar's pearl.
The blood of Bappa Rawal spurned
To yield the prize for which he burned,
But, life to save, allowed his eyes

To look just once upon that prize.
Frankly on Rajput faith reposing,
He came within our fortress, saw
The mirror's face her face disclosing,
And straight returned. So by our law
Of trust for trust and host and guest,
Who on each other's honour rest,
Bheemsi descended to the plain
To see the King take bridle rein.
There foemen set in ambuscade
The lofty Rajput's trust betrayed
And bore him hence with speed. The Khan,
Perfidious like a base Pathan,
Sent challenge that to set him free
Padmani must his ransom be.
So, after counsel, guile with guile
To meet, the Rajputs answer sent

The pearl thus caught by treacherous wile
Would pass unto the monarch's tent
Attended like a queen, and pay
The ransom for her lord. That day
Seven hundred covered litters bore
Her train of handmaids from Chitor,
Each carried by six men. Alas!
Fate adverse saved the Emperor.
The warriors in those litters fought
Like demons, and mowed down like grass
The legions round him ere they sought
The mansions of the Sun. They freed
The Rajput chieftain, and a steed
Whose feet were as the lightning flashing
Carried him safely home, as crashing
Upon that outer gate there came
In hot pursuit a wall of flame,

A sea of steel, and hosts of hell,
On which our heroes clashed and fell.
Tho' ancient bards have said that then
We lost perchance eight thousand men,
We kept brave Bheemsi and his queen
And beat back the false Allah-ud-din.
'Twas some time after, months and more,
Before the tyrant sacked Chitor;
But tho' that day we drove him back,
We count the slaughter half a sack.[3]

[1] Padmíni in Sanskrit, but commonly called Padmani in Méwar.

[2] According to Tod, Bheem Singh, an uncle of the Rana, was the husband of Padmani. Another account assigns her to Ratun Singh, the Rana's brother.

[3] Though the city was not stormed, the best and bravest were cut off (*saka*), A.D. 1303.

II

THE SUTTEE OF GORAH'S WIFE

GORAH and Bádal, the Chauhans, and kin
To fair Padmani, that fierce onslaught led.
Bádal, a boy, was wounded ; Gorah dead,
Covered with wounds and honour, was brought in
And laid upon the pyre, while drums made din.

His wife, the spirit of the Rajput glowing
Within her breast that swelled with love and pride,
Questioned the boy of how her lord had died ;
What glories crowned his coming and his going ?

"Mother," the lad replied—"as reapers reap
The wheat so he the harvest of the battle;
And I who followed 'mid the noise and rattle
Gleaned in the wake of his terrific sweep.
Before he laid him down to rest and sleep

He spread a carpet of the slain upon
The gory bed of honour, made a prince
His pillow, rested joyfully, and since
Unto the mansions of the Sun has gone."
"I know," she cried—"what more? go on! go on!

Tell me again about my love, I pray."
He said, "What further, mother, can I tell?
He left no foe to dread or praise."
"Farewell,"
She smiled, "my lord will chide me for delay"—
Sprang on the pyre, and with him passed away.

III

THE FIRST AND SECOND SACK

'TWAS nigh six hundred years ago
  The Fortress fell, and all our power
Was weakened by the vengeful blow
  That shattered Méwar's bloom and flower.

But when the Tartar seized his prey
  The fruits of conquest had no taste;
No life was there to vex or slay,
  He entered on a barren waste.

The Rana with eleven sons
  And all our males had fallen in fight;
A caverned mine the ashes held
  Of those who ere the Johur[1] rite

Were wives and daughters; all embraced
  The fire, and since no lignt or air
Has pierced the gloom which shrouds their dust.
  Padmani's dust is treasured there.

Bheem's palace and her rooms upon
  The lake within it still were left;
What else? The conqueror made a wreck
  And coldly handed it bereft

Of all our monuments of art
  Unto a slave, the Jhalore chief:
Our Rana's one surviving son
  Nursed in the mountains' depths his grief.

And while he reigned the foreign yoke
  Pressed on the land. By Fate's decree
His son to Deccan exile sent
  Was ancestor to Sivaji,

Who founded the Sattara throne
  And that at Delhi overturned.
When Hamir was our chief the plains
  And villages laid bare and burned

By raids from mountain holds so galled
  The vassal Maldeo in Chitor
He sought alliance : Hamir took
  His daughter unto wife and swore

By hook or crook his grandsire's rock
  Should see the Standard of the Sun
Shine from it once again. He kept
  His oath ; and when the deed was done

The Ghilji Mahmood marching down
  Gave battle by the Chambal ; he
Was put to rout and lodged forsooth
  A prisoner in this Fort for three

Whole months. Then liberty he bought
By a large ransom—fifty lakhs,
With elephants ; and Ranthambor,
Ajmere, Nagore surrendered. Tax

So glorious brought homage free
From Marwar, Jeypore, and each clan
From Gwalior to Abuji.
Méwar was great thro' Hindusthan.

What names, for jewels on her brow,
Like Hamir, Lákha, Chonda, he
Who built the column here to tell
Of many a splendid victory ;

Raised forts around and temples grand
  At Ábu, Sádri; gave his name
To Kumulmer, the Rahtore spoused,
  And after fifty years of fame

Was killed by his own son? Had such
  As these, and Prithi Raj the brave,
Sanga, whom even Báber feared,
  Remained our citadel to save,

Bahadur Sultan had not stormed
  Its walls:[2] again in proud despair
The awful Johur had not claimed
  Our dearest dear, our fairest fair.

'Tis said that thirteen thousand passed
In flame, and thousands thirty-two
Of Rajput warriors of all clans
In that fierce fight were slain and slew.

O strange for Báber's son to be
Our *Rákhi bhai*[3] in time of need!
The captor heard his horses' hoofs
And fled—would God had given them speed!

A fortnight sooner, and Chitor
Had 'scaped that second awful sack;
For when he came a wilderness
To Bikramjeet was given back.

Unworthy thou, O Bikramjeet,
  Of Rana Sanga thy great sire,
Who led the chiefs of Rajasthan
  And raised our banner ever higher.

His name Humáyun's succour gained,
  While thine—but barbed is iron Fate.
Chitor restored, few years shall pass
Before Humáyun's son, alas!
  Shall thunder at its gate.

[1] The last act of a Rajput garrison in extremity was to immolate by fire all their females, to prevent their falling into the hands of the enemy. This rite was called the Johur. See Note, p. 208.

[2] Bahadur Shah, Sultan of Guzerat, took Chitor in A.D. 1534.

[3] See Note, p. 211.

IV

THE THIRD SACK (A.D. 1568) AND AFTER

MAHÁDEO[1] sent us Ooda. He knows best—
For what know we? But cursèd for all time
Is Ooda's name in Méwar: his the crime
Of killing Kumbhu, whom Rajwarra blest.

He snatched the throne before his time, and found
His nobles and his kindred stood afar
And shuddered: so he gave Marwar
Ajmere and Sambhur—ay, and roods of ground

Ancestral, Jodha thus to make his friend.
  The Deora prince in Abu who had known
  Our yoke as vassal he let rule alone.
And e'er remorse pursued him to his end

He offered Delhi (his last gift of shame)
  A daughter for a bride. Then Heaven to save
  The house of Bappa Rawal struck the slave
By lightning—and we never name his name.

But Heaven perchance remembered Ooda's crimes
  When Guzerat avenged them on Chitor.
  Yet all that sacrifice, those seas of gore,
Sufficed not to appease in after times

The wrath of that dread Goddess who aye craved
Princes for victims,[2] and from Bikramjeet
Wrested the throne. The Bastard in his seat
Lost it by pride; and when the *chaonwar*[3] waved

O'er Oodey Singh once more Méwar was glad.
Ah, short-lived joy! In vain the faithful nurse
Doomed her own child,[4] alas! to bring a curse
To manhood. Bappa's line had had

Its good and evil, never once before
A coward: woman's sway had bred
Water in blood. No regal victim led
When mighty Ákbar thundered on Chitor.

So the great goddess hid her face—e'en tho'
  Jaimul and Patta, whom Akbar carved in stone,
  Bédla, Madária, brothers of the throne,
And chiefs of other clans, whose names still glow

In song, put on the saffron [5] for last deed.
  Patta of Kélwa, boy of scarce sixteen,
  Had bride and mother, but with dauntless mien
Each seized a lance and when his turn to lead

Came, rushed on with him, with him fought and fell.
  Only for Ooda four inglorious years
  After that harvest, when the conqueror's spears
And axes shattered this proud citadel

Which thirty thousand died to save. Thereafter,
  Its goddess fled, the wilderness you see
  Remained, and Oodey's city came to be
Our capital. Here every stone and rafter

Of the old ruin has a tale. Once more
  After great Pertap, Oodey's son, cast down
  And hunted, turned and brought renown,
Reconquering all—Amra, his son, Chitor

Regained for a short space ; but times soon changed.
  Rajwarra tore her entrails ; our own fiefs
  And vassals blossomed into minor chiefs,
Servants of Delhi. Peace was then arranged,

And Amra's heir upon the Emperor's right
    Sat at Ajmere: our barons ranked before
    All others—but supremacy was o'er.
No longer sun, but only satellite,

The Rana Karan [6] took from Shah Jahan
    Leave to repair this Fort. 'Twas in his time,
    While Jagat Singh was still in boyhood's prime,
That thro' Chitor men came from Inglistan.

(That Jagat Singh who built the palaces
    Jagmander, Jagnewas, upon the lake
    Pichola.) Then when Arung tried to break
Our hearts and faith, made friends of enemies,

Ambér [7] and Marwar once more at our side,[8]
What glory might have fallen on the land
And made the lotus of our love expand
Had only Rajasthan remained allied!

Thro' her own quarrels crept in the sly fox,
Soon to become a wolf. We could not see
How, worst of all, the race of Sivaji
Would eat up all our goodly lands and flocks:

That Chitor would look down with helpless eyes
On the Mahratta camped beneath her walls,
Thirsting to spoil the jewels and bright halls
Of Oodeypore: [9] and that his robberies [10]

Would last a century and leave Méwar
Beggared of almost all but her past fame—
Till the red coats and the white faces came,
And once again uprose her fortune's star.

[1] The Creative Power, the Great God.

[2] See Note, p. 213.

[3] When a chief appears in state, a *chaonwar*, or yak's tail, is waved slowly over his head by an attendant behind, and, like the umbrella, is one of the insignia of royalty.

[4] See Note, p. 217.

[5] "When a Rajput is determined to hold out to the last in fighting, he always puts on a robe dyed in saffron."—Tod, vol. i. p. 196.

[6] See Note, p. 218.

[7] The ancient appellation of the state now called Jeypore, the city of which name was founded by the great Jey Singh in A.D. 1728.

[8] See Note, p. 218.

[9] In A.D. 1768-69 Oodeypore was besieged by Sindhia for more than a year. The siege was raised on Méwar paying over 60 lakhs and ceding four districts, which, though nominally only mortgaged, have never been recovered.

[10] Tod is very eloquent on the subject of these robberies. See his *Annals of Méwar:* "When, in A.D. 1795, a marriage was negotiated between the Rana's sister and the prince of Jeipoor, the Rana was obliged to borrow £50,000 from the Mahratta commander Umbaji to purchase the nuptial presents."

KRISHNA KUMÁRI

A.D. 1805

O BEAUTIFUL as moonlight
Were her virtues and her grace,
And her fame was like the sunlight,
For the whole world praised her face
As a rose of Gulistan at
Which the wild bee honey sips,
And flower of the pomegranate
Was the blossom of her lips!

Ah! that was Krishna, Flower of Rajasthan,
Whom Ajit and the robber Amir Khan
(He rose from being a common thief,
God help us, to a ruling chief)
Did—and we curse them in one breath
For that foul doing—did to death.
The tale, wherever it is known,
Must move methinks a heart of stone.

A princess of the purest race,
Her matchless form, her peerless face,
Were sung abroad in town and camp,
Till, like a moth unto the lamp,
Came Jeypore, suitor for her hand;
And Jodhpore after made demand.
Sindhia's hard yoke was on the land,
And he, to wound a father's heart

And Jagat Singh's, took Marwar's part.
So Jeypore's presents were returned,
And half Rajwarra raged and burned.
Love rang out war's wild, shrill, alarms
As fiery rivals flashed to arms.

A mighty army gleaned each field
And ate up all Marwar could yield :
But Jodha's castle scorned attack.
So Jagat Singh perforce, for lack
Of food and forage, journeyed back.

His friend and ally Amir Khan,
True ally, sworn on the Koran,
Exchange of turbans, and what not,
Bribed by the foe, his oath forgot—
And fell upon his friend's worn host
(Let Tonk of that proud victory boast !)

Thus crowned with infamy this thief
Sought Oodeypore and stormed our Chief
With threats, if Krishna were not given
To Raja Mán, or else to Heaven.
Ajit, Chandáwat, then had ear
Of Rana Bheem Singh full of fear,
And he, base coward, thro' design
For self and ill to Bappa's line,
Advised, to end the bloody strife,
The sacrifice of Krishna's life.
Dowlat was asked to use the knife
To save the honour of the clan,
But answered like a true brave man,
" If this be honour, faith is dead,
Dust on my loyalty and head."
Then Jawan Dás, of her own blood,
Before the youthful victim stood

To slay—but quickly turned and fled.
Her virgin innocence and shield
Of beauty suddenly revealed
Horror of guilt that might appal
The hardest heart: so he let fall
The dagger in his hand.
But cries
For mercy, tears from mother's eyes,
The mother who had seen the knife
And loved her daughter more than life,
Availed not; tho' the steel was spared,
Women the poisoned cup prepared,
And brought to Krishna in the name
Of her weak father, bowed by shame,
Amir and Ajit. Calm she drank
And said, to soothe with love and pride
The frantic mother at her side,

"O mother dearest, let me thank
My father I have lived so long:
Weep not, for I have done no wrong.
Am I not your own daughter dear?
Why death should Rajput princess fear?
Does it not end our sorrows here?
What joy is there to us on earth,
Marked out for sacrifice from birth?"

The poison would not stay—tho' thrice
She drank, the lovely sacrifice
Was not complete till a fourth draught,
With opium added, had been quaffed.
She slept: and quickly anguish deep
Brought the reft mother the same sleep.

Words never told so dark a crime
  As that which closed thy sixteen years

And killed thy mother in her prime :

The tale is all too deep for tears,
Too sorrowful to dwell upon,
Krishna Kumari, past and gone !

AT NÁTHDWÁRA[1]

SACRED to Rajasthan the place which shrines
  The image of that Krishna deified
A thousand years and more—'tis said, from signs
  And texts which learnèd persons have descried—

Before our Christ: Nathdwara is its name.
  The image was at Mathura until,
Proscribed by Aurangzeb, 'twas saved from shame
  Thro' Rana Raj, by whose protecting will

The Rajputs brought it to Méwar on wheels
  Which at this spot sank deep in earth and none
Could move them. "Thus," they said, "the god reveals
  His wish to dwell here." So the town begun.

Maharana Bhima Singhji gave a grant,[2]
  Thro' the chief butler, of such lands and dues
And privileges to the hierophant
  That what he asks no man may dare refuse.

Pope of Rajwarra is this priest; for "he
  Who doth resume that grant," men know full well
'Tis writ, "for sixty thousand years will be
  A caterpillar in the depths of hell."

[1] *Dwára* (portal), *Nàth* (god).

[2] For translation of this grant see Note, p. 219.

THE RAHTORES[1]

AT JODHPORE 1890

A local bard is supposed to be addressing an English traveller

IN far Kanauj, the cradle of our race,
  God knows how many centuries it ruled,
  Till, broken and by hard misfortune schooled,
A handful of our brave went forth to face
  The dangers of this desert, then a sheer
  Waste without tilth or township. Well, 'tis near
  Seven hundred years since then and Seoji,
  And four since Jodha raised the fort you see.

The mausoleums standing at Mundore,
Our ancient capital, contain much lore
About the fortunes of the bold Rahtore.
You may have read how, with Méwar, he strove
Against the Moghal Baber, and had won,
But for mean treachery, which he does not love.
Ah! that and fierce disunion have undone
Rajwarra many a time, until the arms
Of Britain leagued with ours dispelled alarms.
For seventy years each State has held its own
In peace since Delhi ceased to make us groan,
And London holds your Queen's imperial throne.
But what a power we had in Maldeo's time,
Three centuries and a half ago!—Nagore,
Ajmere, Serohi—ay, and many a prime
Slice of what now is Tonk, Méwar, Jeypore.
He lorded Bika's city. Had he sent

Aid to Humáyun on his weary flight,
The babe which first at Umerkote saw light,
An angry mother nursing discontent,
Had not deflowered his conquests. But who knows?
The tide of Destiny remorseless flows.
How could he read that babe's auspicious star
And say, "This Akbar will invade Marwar"—[2]
Or tell that ere his seven-and-thirty-year
Dominion ceased, not only Bikanir
Would fall away, but, many a rich prize lost,
Over our famed *Panchranga*, tempest-tossed,
Would float proud Akbar's banner: that his son
Would serve the Emperor, a daughter give
In marriage to prolong the Moghal line,
And take from Delhi leave to rule and live—
"King of the Desert," "Oodey Singh the Fat"?
Maldeo took leave from none; but after that

Times changed: Rajwarra, by great Akbar's wiles
And her own feuds divided, grew more tame,
Saw fame and fortune in a conqueror's smiles,
Her bravest leaders banished under name
Of viceroys in the Deccan and elsewhere,
Her own blood mixed with Moghal's. Yet where'er
The Rahtore went his valour in the air
Flashed like a sword, and evermore the same.
Nor Malwa, Deccan, Guzerat, nor snows
Of Kabul, tide of luck that sank or rose,
Moghal, Mahratta, nor the Frenchman's [4] guns
Could chill the fire of Jodha's noble sons.

[1] See Note, p. 220.

[2] Marwar is a corruption of Maroo-war, classically Maroost'hali or Maroost'han, "the region of death." The bards frequently style it Mord'hur, which is synonymous with Maroo-désa, or, when it suits their rhyme, simply Maroo. Though now restricted to the country subject to the Rahtore race, its ancient and appropriate application comprehended the entire desert from the Sutlej to the ocean.—Tod's *Rajasthan*.

[3] The five-coloured flag of the Rajputs.

[4] De Boigne, Sindhia's famous general, who won his chief victories.

AMRA SINGH

THINK of Gaj Singh, his father Raja Soor,
Amra and Jeswant his two sons: those four
Were specimens in truth of the Rahtore—
Bad in the blood he may be, never poor.

You've heard of Amra? Fire was in his veins.
The Deccan knew it: many a glorious fight
Attested there the fury of his might.
But when it came his turn to hold the reins

As chief of Maroo, somehow there was fear;
Which ended in his brother being seated
Upon the *gadi*, and his going from here [1]
Hotter than ever, ready for affray

With man or tiger. Soon there came a day
When, careless of the Emperor, who had cheated
His hopes, he made continual neglect
Of service such as emperors expect:
Whereat the World's King fumed to be obeyed,
Threatened a fine; bold Amra, unafraid,
Replied his fortune lay in his sword-blade.
So anger filled the soul of Shah Jahan.
To take the fine he sent Salabat Khan
With speed: the Bakshi [2] hurried back much faster
With words of insult carried to his master.

Then Amra, summoned to a full durbar,
Strode swiftly past each wondering *mansabdar* [3]
Up to the Presence, and with one quick dart
Buried his dagger in Salabat's heart.
The next blow nearly fell upon the King,

Who fled—a pillar marked the dagger's swing.
And ere the Rahtore's work and life were done
Five Ameers sought the mansions of the Sun;
While his retainers, clad in saffron, drew
Their swords on all around and hacked and slew.

Thus Amra entered Amrapura,[4] mad
With rage: Champáwat and Kumpáwat, glad
To avenge on Moghal enemy his fate,
Rushed also with him thro' that city's gate.
Last, his brave Bundi Queen, to prove her clan
Of Rajput womanhood not less than man,
Bore her lord's body from that carnage dire
And passed with it upon the funeral pyre.

1 See Note, p. 222.

2 Paymaster of the troops.

3 "Of the 416 *mansabdars*, or military commanders, of Akbar's empire, from leaders of 200 to 10,000 men, 47 were Rajputs, and the aggregate of their quotas amounted to 53,000 horse."—Tod, vol. i. p. 153.

4 An immortal abode.

AJIT SINGH

A.D. 1680-1725

JESWANT was cool where Amra was aflame.
    A ruler needs must fence ; but no one hated
The Moghal more. Great was his martial fame,
    Fighting at first for Dara the ill-fated
By the Nerbudda, after in the south,
    And last at Kabul. Aurangzeb the King,
Who cast his arrows with a smiling mouth
    And lies like honey, kept brave Jeswant Singh
Afar from Maroo. Forty years our Chief,
    But ever viceroy in some distant clime,
Until he died at Kabul, bowed with grief ;

His only son a martyr in life's prime
By poison and the tyrant. "Arung's [1] sighs
Ceased not while Jeswant lived," our bards have sung:
But after Jeswant *swerga* [2] gained, the young
Ajit was born to him; and this, the prize
And hope of Maroo-désh, a gallant band
Of Rahtores bringing from that northern land,
Was stayed at Delhi by the King's command.
"Give up the child," he said, "and you shall share
His birthright." Faithful to their trust they made
Reply. Surrounded by a host they quaffed
The last deep draught of opium,[3] and laughed
Defiance to false Arung's fiendish craft.

The infant prince was first by stealth conveyed,
Hid in a basket, by a Meah [4] true,
Who safely passed the Moghal ambuscade.

Then the Rahtores their wives and daughters drew
Into a room where gunpowder was laid.
The torch applied, those grim old warriors, free
From care, sang each to other joyfully—

Let us swim in the ocean of fight
To the mansions of the Sun;
We have lived and fought in the sight
Of our lord whose battles are done;
And we fear no Islamite
Tho' he be as fifty to one.

The star of a tyrant abhorred
To-day may be in ascendant;
Shall we kneel and feast from his board,
On his bounty be dependent?
We have tasted the gifts of our lord,
And will make his salt resplendent.

Let the music of sword and shield
Begin for the brave Rahtore,
His blood shall flow as on field
Of renown his fathers' before.
Let his eyes by sleep be sealed,
He shall wake in Chandrapore.[5]

No man might look to ride thro' such a host,
But Govind[6] smiled. Heroic Doorga Dàs
(A name for evermore our country's boast,
His virtues those of gods above surpass),
With a choice few our Jeswant's child regains,
And speeds once more towards Maroo's sandy plains.
But war is all around: for safety's sake
To sacred Abu Maroo's Hope they take,
And there in secret among monks, unknown
His birth, they rear him for his father's throne.

But six-and-twenty years must pass of war
Such as was never waged in days before,
Thousands of Rajputs *swerga's* mansions swell,
And lakhs of Moslems grind their teeth in hell,
And Arung there the *nuzzer*[7] of their curses
Receive[8]—ay, victories, reverses
Must pass in shoals ere Jodhpore once again
Proclaim her Ajit lord of all the plain.

Did Arung dream that Jeswant's babe, concealed
And borne by Meah true, thro' hand of Fate
Which conquers all, would one day wave the shield
Of triumph, thundering at his palace gate—
Make and unmake the World's King, take Ajmere,
And reign from Sambhur Lake to Jesalmere?
Yet so it came. Had Akbar lived, Chauhan,
Sesodia, Hára, Bhattia, Rajasthán

With all her tribes, had not combined his power
(For it was wise) to crush, e'en for an hour.

But Arung thrust his Islam down our throats,
  Shattered our idols ;[9] so when Lord Ajit
Crested the wave and sank the bigot's boats,
  He made the Rahtore's lordship so complete
That rites of Islam not a soul might dare
To practise, and in Maroo everywhere
Dread silence held the Moslem's call to prayer.

This same Ajit (the ways of Fate are deep !)
  Exiled brave Doorga Dàs, his staunchest friend ;
And by his own son murdered in his sleep,
  His splendid reign was brought to sudden end.

Epilogue

'Twas Ajit's daughter given to Ferokhsir
  In marriage at the Court of Delhi led,
If I may say so, to your presence here.
  For while the nuptials, as you may have read,
Were going on, upon the Emperor fell
  A sickness, which an English doctor's skill
Soon cured; and so the marriage went off well.
  The Emperor, grateful, signified his will
To let the doctor name his own reward;
And he, instead of asking for a hoard
Of silver, sought a firmán for a friend
To start a factory—which in the end
Became a town, Calcutta—brought your Clive
And Warren Hastings. Thus a single hive

Of bees that looked for honey, stinging, slowly
Spread over Hindusthan, and merchants lowly
Built up the empire of your Empress Queen.
That is how Ajit's daughter on the scene
Comes in.

But as for Doctor Hamilton,
I never heard that anything was done
For him. Clive has a statue—he has none.[10]

1 In the language of the bards Aurangzeb is always "Arung."

2 Paradise.

3 This draught was the usual prelude to death or victory in fight.

4 A term of respect applied to a Mahomedan, imputing respectability and experience.

5 City of the Moon.

6 Krishna—the supreme deity.

7 A gift presented in token of homage or respect.

8 Aurangzeb died A.D. 1707.

9 See Note, p. 222.

10 Tod remarks: "To borrow the phraseology of the Italian historian, 'obligations which do not admit of being fully discharged are often repaid with the coin of ingratitude'; the remains of this man rest in the churchyard of Calcutta, without even a stone to mark the spot."

THE FOUNDING OF BIKANIR, A.D. 1489

Bika, son of Jodha, addresses the Godarra and Roneah Jits

O PATRIARCHS of the desert, ye have heard
    Of Jodha and the kingdom he hath won ;
Strength of the lion, swiftness of the bird,
    Hath Bika the Rahtore, brave Jodha's son.
Your clans are warring, ye have suffered long,
Roneah, Godarra, I will make you strong.

Ye fear your kindred Jits, ye dread the band
    Of Bhattis plundering from Jesalmere—

Fear not, my arm and name shall shield your land
  And cause your enemies in truth to fear.
Here will I build a city, ay, and make
The wilderness to blossom for your sake.

Whose is this land? The plot of Néra Jit—
  And he will have my city bear his name?
Well said, my friends, his name and mine shall meet
  And bring him and your country endless fame.
We will set up a noble city here
On this high ground and call it Bikanir.

Your rights and privileges are secure:
  I guard them ever as I would mine own.
Nay, while the line of Bika shall endure,
  I promise none shall e'er ascend the throne
Till ye have set the *tika*[1] on his brow.
So, that is done. Your foes are my foes now.

I am your Chief: ye know my destiny
 Karniji at Deshnúk some years ago
Foretold;[2] she hath the seer's prophetic eye.
 Have I not routed Bhattis? Yea, ye know
What I have done; 'tis not for me to say.
But you shall see what I will do one day.

[1] "The unguent of royalty." See Note, p. 223.

[2] "On reaching Deshnúk, 16 miles south of the present city of Bikanir, he paid his respects to a famous Charan woman named Karniji, who was known to be gifted with supernatural power. She said to him, "Your destiny is higher than your father's and many servants will touch your feet."—Powlett's *Gazetteer of Bikanir.*

A RAJA'S DYING BEQUEST[1]

BIKANIR, A.D. 1611

MY sons, in Akbar Badshah's reign
  (May God confound him and his line!)
There was a varlet in my train
  At Court to whom the King would sign
When I was present, make him sit
  While I was standing, and play chess.
'Twas thus he sharpened sour wit
  Upon the Rajput: and thro' stress
Of circumstance I had to smile
  And Akbar's condescension thank:
My fierce blood boiling all the while
  At such an insult to my rank.

So I resolved it should go hard
  With that same base-born dog whose fame
At chess had won the King's regard.
  " He shall pay dearly for his game
When we get back to Bikanir,"
  Methought ; but somehow thro' some fate
Unkind the fellow scented fear
  (He was the Dewan of the State)
And fled to Delhi. (Those who let
  The hound escape you may be sure
My royal wrath did not forget.)
  Well, there he prospered, and no lure
Could tempt him back. When Akbar died
  Jahangir Badshah called me. Then
This Karam Chand Bacháwat's pride
  (I hated him above all men)
Was humbled by the hand of Death.

I saw him dying, and my tears
Deceived his sons ; but his last breath
Revived, 'tis said, their slumbering fears.
He warned them that I wept to see
Him dying undisgraced, and told
Them never to return to me.
In vain my grief with theirs condoled,
That warning stuck.
Now I am dying
All unavenged on him and his :
I charge you therefore, cease not trying
By all the wiles of Nemesis
To lure Bacháwats here once more.
And when they come—good boys and true,
Remembering that slight of yore,
You know what I would have you do.

[1] Raja Rai Singh, who ruled in Bikanir from A.D. 1571 to A.D. 1611.

THE SEQUEL

Praise be to God! I, Soor Singh
When paying homage to the King,
Succeeded where my father failed.
By solemn promise I prevailed
On Karam Chand's two sons to share
The office that their father bare.

Honoured as Dewans to their side
Bacháwats flocked and triumph cried,
Believing that my father's son
Rejoiced o'er ancient wrong undone.
They sunned themselves in Fortune's beam.
Two months I let them dream their dream,
Then swooped upon them with one bound.
Four thousand soldiers hemmed them round.

The day of vengeance broke at last—
And so they met their fate, and passed.

The dogs ground up their jewels, killed
Their women—ay, and good blood spilled
Of Rajput warriors, but not one
Lived to behold the setting sun.
I had them in a pretty fix—
For what can one man do 'gainst six?

Their homes laid bare, I made that place
For evermore a black disgrace
To Karam Chand and all his race.
'Tis peopled by the Bojaks[1] now.
So I fulfilled my father's vow.
Praise be to God that I his son
Have done what he would fain have done!

[1] Jain temple-sweepers.

RAJA KARAN SINGH OF BIKANIR

A.D. 1639-1669

PROEM

YOU know how two guns more or less
  In the case of a Raja's salute
Will lead him to ban or to bless,
  And how very important to boot
Is the distance you go to receive
  A Chief, and the place of his seat.
And yet you may hardly believe
  The story I'm going to repeat.
Bikaniris still tell it with pride
  To show what their Rajas could do ;

And unless their historians have lied
  It is all undeniably true.
Other States may say it is not,
  Or set it aside with a laugh
As a joke at the end of a plot,
  A comedy acted in chaff.
This reading, however, is scouted
  By bards who punctilio revere
And won't for a moment have flouted
  The dignity of Bikanir.[1]

A bard of Bikanir is supposed to be speaking to an Englishman

Soor Singh was great, but Karan Singh his son
Did what no man in Rajasthan has done;
Made its proud chiefs acknowledge him as first,
Bow down to him in durbar (how they cursed!).

This was the way it came about. His sons
Késri and Padam Singh were brave in fight,
And when Prince Dara fought for his own right
And lost, they were among the lucky ones
Who won. The Emperor, so people say,
Brushed from their clothes the dust of battle—yea,
With his own hand: great honour: he became
Their friend and Karan Singh's. But all the same
The crafty Aurangzeb, religion-mad,
Broke up the temples at our sacred places
Benares and Brindában, led our races
To war beyond the Indus River, had
Contrived a scheme when on the other side
To humble our religion and our pride,
Our Hindusthan to bend upon her knee
To Islam; Akbar's tolerant policy
Reversing thus. The bigot's secret plan

Was whispered to the chiefs of Rajasthan.
Their rage was like the ocean in a storm,
Their fears were as the snows on Caucasus;
So to dissemble and in cunning form
Escape the Emperor's friendship tortuous
Seemed wise. To cross the flood were ready then
A thousand boats and more; we sent our men
To seize them for our crossing *first*. "But nay,"
Cried all the Islamites (a legion they
Beside our troops), "we cross, O friends, then you."
That they would say this, well our Rajas knew.
That was the trick; for when the stream so wide
Was passed, our forces on the hither side,
And all the boats sent back, it was agreed
They should be broken. Who would take the lead
In such a task? The assembled Rajas said,
"O Karan Singh, your country last need dread

The tyrant's vengeance ; he in truth might fear
To plough the boundless sands of Bikanir.
Therefore be yours to dc this daring deed,
We helping, and when done let's homeward speed."
So said, so done : but Raja Karan Singh
Named one condition—" I will do this thing
If seated on my throne you pass to-day
Before me, all of you, and homage pay."
The chiefs of Rajasthan were ill content,
But in the end they yielded their assent.
So in durbar our prince was hailed as chief.[2]
We mark the story as a golden leaf
In our State annals, and may well reply,
When others boast, that Bikanir ranks high.

What did the Emperor do? You may suppose
His wrath at finding that we had retreated

And seeing all his dark design defeated.
'Twas told him Karan Singh was first of those
Who led retreat, and how that he had rent
The boats in pieces: therefore on return
To Delhi was an army straightway sent
To march on Bikanir and slay and burn.
Ah! then our chief, remembering in distress
That piety is good and saints can bless,
Turned to Karniji at her Deshnúk shrine
And through entreaty won a grace divine.
For lo, the army by some sudden thought
Of Aurangzeb's was back to Delhi brought.
There came a summons to brave Karan Singh,
And scorning fear he went to face the King.
"Let the worst fall," he said, "the Moghal's eye
Shall see a Rajput does not quail to die!"

In cloth of gold and jewels bright arrayed
  The Badshah of the World (they called him so)
Sat in his hall of audience. Diamonds made
  The sunlight dim, but e'en that durbar's glow,
Tho' it outshone the star beside the pole,
Was darkened by the murder in his soul:
For he had ordered that brave Karan's life
Should pass in durbar by the assassin's knife.
The plot was ripe; but suddenly the King
Beheld beside their father Késri Singh
And Padam Singh, those famous men who fought
His battles against Dara, and the thought
That Késri Singh had saved his life uprising
Leapt from his lips. On which wise Karan Singh
Exclaimed, "The victory of my lord the King
Was due to his own piety surprising—
He read the Koran all throughout the fight."

Whereat the Emperor changed his former spite
(The butchers read his sign), and purposed then
Not to destroy but use such gallant men.
So Karan Singh was spared, thro' his brave lad,
And sent on service to Aurangabad.
And there he died long after, having founded
The village Karanpura and surrounded
It with pán gardens. There a temple too
He built unto our saint Karniji, who
Had saved and guided him all perils through.

Saiyads in Bikanir—you ask me how
They came. 'Twas Karan Singh who brought them. First
Was one who in that tale I told just now
Revealed the Emperor's design accursed

To stamp out our religion. Him our lord
  Granted a village free of rent and gave
A pice on every house ('twas good reward)
  In Bikanir. And since the seed of brave
And faithful Saiyads grew. They serve us fair,
  And are not like Mahomedans elsewhere.

[1] See Note, p. 224, for another anecdote of punctilio also told in Powlett's *Gazetteer of Bikanir*.

[2] In Bikanir it is stated that he was saluted as king of the jungle, and the present Maharaja's note-paper bears under a device or crest the inscription, "*Jai, jungal dhar badsha*" (Triumph, king of the jungle!).

RAJA GAJ SINGH OF BIKANIR TO RAJA BIJEY SINGH OF JODHPORE[1]

AT JEYPORE, A.D. 1764

WE little thought, my friend, our host
Was fooling us with elephant fights
And fountains playing, feasts and sights
And dancing girls. What riles me most
Is—not the time in waiting lost
To hear if he would send his aid
To guard your fort against the raid
Of those Mahrattas who are round it
And growing much too strong—confound it!

What vexes me is this—that he,
After recalling many a year
Of friendship 'twixt his house and mine,
And saying that he wished to see
Those villages of Bikanir
Which Ajit Singh unjustly took
And you would rather not resign,
Returned to me—should secretly
Propose that you be brought to book,
Not by persuasion, friendship's claims,
Which no one of our kindred blames,
But by a dungeon's walls, or worse,
The assassin's knife. It is the curse
Of all our houses that such tricks
Should be so common. I refused
To have my friend so badly used,
On which Jeypore himself excused,

Saying he must go talk to you.
Suspecting treachery in the wind,
At once I bade my trusty two
Follow the crafty one behind.

The rest you know; how in durbar
He rose and was about to go—
The signal for some sharp *tulwar*,
Nay fifty, to divide your spine—
When those two followers of mine
Sprang up and caught Maharaja by
The girdle and most courteously
Requested him to sit and show
Their fears were groundless. But one blow
At you and he was a dead man,
And I his foe. He saw my plan—
And understood it. What is more,

He honoured as a chieftain can
The courage of the bold Rahtore[2]—
Who else had dared to stop such wrong?
Our bards at home shall make a song
That thro' the ages loud shall ring
In praise of Pem and Hathi Singh.

But now, my friend, let us away.
I'll see you out of this. Some day
This courtesy you may repay.

[1] With reference to this and the next Rhyme, see Note, p. 225.

[2] The Maharaja forbade any attack on them, "and Bijai Singh, at the suggestion of the two Bikanir Thakurs, withdrew, joined Gaj Singh, and they both returned to their camp; Pem Singh and Hathi Singh remaining behind to apologise and give up their swords to Madho Singh, whom they declared they honoured as their master. They readily obtained the forgiveness of Madho Singh, who permitted the two chiefs to depart on hostages being given for the performance of Gaj Singh's promise to return after seeing Bijai Singh across the boundary."—Powlett's *Gazetteer of Bikanir.*

BIJEY SINGH TO GAJ SINGH

AT NÁTHDWARA, A.D. ABOUT 1770

YOU were my father's friend—alas
That on his name there rests that stain!
E'en gifts to Brahmans are in vain
For guilt of parricide to pass.
You know he did the deed to raise
His brother Abhey Singh, and how
They quarrelled—and in after days
How Abhey tried a force to bring
Against my sire Bakhtawar Singh,
And would have crumpied you as well.

There is no need for me to tell
My father's friend and mine how Fate
Has linked our fortunes, nor relate
How his strong arm has added weight
To mine. We have been close allies.
And rest assured that I do prize
The honourable aid you lent
(Would all my friends were as well-bred !)
That time when like a fool I went,
Trusting to Honour's risky laws,
And put my very foolish head
Into the Jeypore tiger's jaws.
The poisoned robe he sent my sire
Should have reminded me to dread
The venom of his treacherous ire.
You got me out of that—and I,
You will remember by-the-bye,

Gave you some villages on which
You'd set your heart, and sent a rich
Donation to Karniji's shrine
At Deshnúk. That is past and gone.
Touching this question you have mooted
I ask you, would you have me hooted?
I see that it would make your name
Still greater if through you Méwar
Regained this district of Godwar
(Though that of course is not your aim),
And I would help you if I could
As far as loyal ally should.
For well you know 'twixt you and me
There is no room for jealousy.
Sprung like myself from Jodha's veins,
No chieftain worthier maintains
His lordship—over desert plains.

As for his learning, I declare
It makes Nathdwara's Gosain stare.
But, O my friend, recall to mind
What I have borne through fate unkind,
Since first we rode in that great fight
When panic cast its fearful blight,
As our own guns by strange mischance
Scattered the finest cavalry
That e'er in Maroo[1] carried lance.
And then a misbegotten lie,
That I the King was low and dead,
Like a fierce jungle fire spread,
And so our armies broke and fled.
You know how that same luckless King,
Charging whole squadrons thro' and thro',
Full many a Rajput's life-blood drew
And many a stout Mahratta slew,

Yet at the last, no succour nigh,
Was forced (O shame!) to turn and fly,
Fly like a bird upon the wing.
Then after that my Thakurs, all
  At feud among themselves, made life
A burden to me. Stop their brawl
  I could not, save by foreign strife.
Therefore it was that Umerkote
  I took, and filched from Jesalmere
A slice—poor conquests, not a groat
  Of gain my treasury to cheer.
Then one bright ray of fortune smiled.
  Méwar, distracted by worse hap
Than mine of Thakurs, like a child
  Placed this rich jewel in my lap
To keep for safety.[2] Safe enough
  It is: now, say you, please restore?

My Thakurs are a trifle rough—
Just put that to them. What a roar
They make! I told you—live, let live.
You see Godwar's not mine to give.

[1] The old name for Marwar—signifies death.

[2] "This district, which was won with the title of Rana from the Purihara, prince of Mundore, before Jodpoor was built, and whose northern boundary was confirmed by the blood of the Chondawut chief in the reign of Joda, was confided by the Rana to the care of Raja Beejy Singh of Jodpoor, to prevent its resources being available to the Pretender, whose residence, Komulmer, commanded the approach to it."—Tod, vol. i. p. 434.

BIJEY SINGH ON HIS DEATH-BED

A.D. 1794[1]

WHO says that victory waited on Ram Singh
And never on my arms? Do they forget
Tonga? We charged the Frenchman at his guns,
Recovered all that Sindhia took from us,
Ay, and redeemed Ajmere. Was that Ram Singh
Or I? Good God! To think that four years afterwards,
Ajmere retaken, the Mahratta yoke
Was heavier than ever on our necks.
Pátan and Mérta—bah! they sicken me,
Those names. Jeypore again: the Kachwaha,

My father's foe and mine, secured himself,
Even when leagued with me against De Boigne.
Alone the Rahtore galloped on those guns—
Our ally had received his price. No wonder
We failed. But worst of all to know our chains
Were riveted at Mérta by a man
Of our own clan—yes—Rahtore—spit upon
His name for evermore—Bahadur Singh,
The chief of Kishengurh. What next? what next?
That breaks my heart. Why, Damraj, in whose veins
Flowed only Rajput bravery, not blood,
When he received my order to deliver
Ajmere, obeyed, but saying, "Let the Southron step
Over my body," swallowed diamond dust.

Alas, 'tis true the fortunes of my house
Have darkened ever, thro' no fault of mine!

The curse, the curse—I seem to hear the bards
Proclaiming at my mausoleum, " Ah !
The Kamdhuj[2] killed his father brave Ajit :
His mother cursed him from the funeral pyre :
Her awful ringing curse, *The murderer's bones*
May they not burn in Maroo, was fulfilled,
And dogged his son for over thirty years
With sad misfortune."

[1] See Note, p. 226.

[2] A titular appellation of the Rahtore kings which they brought from Kanauj.

AT JESALMERE[1]

WHO would have dreamt in such a waste of sand
To find such art in carven work of stone?
A castle worthy of an ancient throne,
And this same art proclaim to all the land
A fallen greatness. Once the roving band
Which Deoraj and Jesal called their own
Grew to possess much territory known
As Bikanir and Marwar since the hand
Which grasped was cold, and evil dogged its days.
The desert tribes were always reivers bold

And fortune swayed as leaders strove to raise
The spoil a weaker gauntlet failed to hold.
Yet bards resound the ancient Bhatti's praise—
The Rajput counts his lineage more than gold.

Famed for its camels, Jesal's city wears
The camel's hue; one colour all around
Save the blue sky. 'Tis strange the desert-bound
The love of fatherland so constant bears
That e'en the Sétt, whose interests and cares
In foreign loans and merchandise are found,
Clings to the home on his ancestral ground
And by the name *Marwari* proudly swears.
It breathes to him the desert air.

By chance
The desert saved this land for many a year
From the Mahratta's desolating lance.

Scourged by the Moslem and by sword and spear
Of its own factions, how the old romance
Reddens with slaughter luckless Jesalmere!

[1] Tod spells the name of the founder as Jessul, and says the site of the town was pointed out by a hermit named Eesul, who stipulated that the fields to the westward of the castle should retain his name. See Note, p. 228.

AT JEYPORE

THE KACHWAHAS

Local guide loquitur

FROM Kush the son of Rama we derive
Kachwa or Kachwaha our tribal name.
There is a word like that which also means
The Tortoise, and sometimes our enemies
Have taunted us with being slow, altho'
They blame us too for being first to give
A daughter to the Delhi Emperor
In marriage: let that pass—the times
Were evil; chiefs and leaders everywhere

Spotted the name of every tribe and state,
And we being nearest to the Delhi throne
Were first o'ershadowed. What of that? The others
Followed soon after—Méwar last of all,
Because 'twas far and lay among the hills.
But if you come to measure chiefs, Mán Singh,
Jey Singh, the Mirza Raja, brave Pratáp,
Will bear comparison in arms, while none,
Nay, not a man in Hindusthan, for science
Could hold a candle to Siwai Jey Singh.
(*Siwai*, or one-and-quarter, was a title
Given to mark that he was head and shoulders
Above the common run of chiefs and men.)
Ambér had been our capital for seven
Long centuries since Hamaji had driven
The Minas from it, but Siwai Jey Singh
Founded and named this city with broad streets

And room to spread in Seventeen Twenty-eight.
So Ambér was deserted—the old place
Slowly has crumbled to a lovely ruin
Delightful to the tourist. Ah! Jey Singh
Was a great man, the Euclid of his day;
Versed in astronomy, observatories
He made in other cities besides this.
Science, the parent of ingenious arts,
Found, if not pupil, patron wise, sagacious,
In our last chief Ram Singh, who left a name
For help to learning, art, and making laws,
For being liberal to the cultivator
In time of famine, which the present chief
Maharaja Madho Singh will not let die.
Look round and see our College, streets with water
Laid on from taps, gas-lighted, see our gardens
And Albert Hall which Colonel Jacob built,

And ask him (for he has been twenty years
Our architect and engineer, bestowing
Blessing around in various ways and making
His name a household word throughout the state),
Ask Dr. Hendley, the authority
On Indian Art, when you have seen the Mayo
Hospital, the museum he created,
And other institutions in the town,
If we deserve the name of Tortoise. Ha!
'Tis a good joke—the State which spends the most
And has the greatest revenue, is first
In education—but I will not boast:
The Rajputs everywhere are brave and strong,
And all of us should use our strength for peace
And fruits of peace. Sir, that is our endeavour.

INFANTICIDE

THE outer world and its fast-changing ways
Is scarce a theme the Rajput loves to praise.
But is there left a man of sword and spear,
Who ties his beard and whisker round each ear,
So wedded to the ancient beaten track
As to desire the days of Suttee back ?
Widows there may be, even children, so
Encompassed by a lifelong doom of woe
That to them stricken the old funeral pyre
Seems mercy thro' its swift release by fire ;
But the strong hand that quenched the death of flame
Is reverenced throughout the land, and shame

Now clings to relics of a country's pride—
What relic worse than girl-infanticide?

The Rajput may not marry in his clan:
A daughter's dower has ruined many a man:
Chárans, or bards, who came to bless or ban
At every marriage feast, than locusts worse,
Beggared the simpletons who feared their curse.[1]
And all were simple; Custom held them down—
Custom, the king who laughs at every crown.
Infanticide was heir to that same king,
And had been conquered by Siwai Jey Singh
Had all the States of Rajasthan agreed
To join the crusade that he tried to lead.
But no, a chief would bear a lifelong load
For Cháran's praise—it might be one brief ode—
And so to pay for marriage song and mirth

The little girls were smothered at their birth.
Jey Singh was wise and counselled a decree
That none should spend on marriage feast and fee
More than his income for a single year;
But old Rajwarra wisdom would not hear,
Or dared not, till, infanticide made crime
By English rule, slow-educating time
And hard experience brought the lesson home
That erst unheeded many a stately home
Had marred. An English ruler found
Seven years ago an hour when men around
Were willing to unite and shake the throne
Of that old custom which had made them groan.
So the society which bears the name
Of Colonel Walter[2] rose, and has done more
Than Jey Singh ever dreamed of; but his aim
Deserves to be linked with it evermore.

After-Thought

Is it a judgment for the crime that wide
Spread the dark guilt of girl-infanticide
That even now for Rajput chief 'tis rare
To be succeeded by a lineal heir?
Look round—how many a throne is filled by one
Adopted, not begotten, as a son!

[1] See Note, p. 229.

[2] This society, known as the Walterkrit Rajputra Hitkarini Sabha, founded in A.D. 1888 when Colonel Walter was Governor-General's Agent in Rajputana, has framed, and is successfully working, with the general consent of all the States, rules whose object is to prevent marriages between Rajputs of immature age, and to restrict expenditure on marriages and funerals, which used to be ruinous.

IN SHEKHAWATI

HERE where the sand is deep a hardy breed
Of men and horses range; 'tis Bikanir
Or Marwar in the face, Jeypore in name,
And tributary to the capital
Of gas and water pipes, in sharp contrast.
Nor loves the brave Shekháwat to recall
That tribute; often he remembers how
A younger son of Ambér, given this land
In appanage and yearning for a son,
Was comforted by prophecy of saint,
A holy man of Islam, Sheikh Burhán—

Which, all fulfilled, gave birth to Sheikhji (named
After the saint) who founded empire free
From yoke of any chief of his own clan.
Nearly five hundred years have passed since then:
And Sheikhji's sons, by cleavage of home feud
Continual, lost the lordship that forsakes
The house divided, ere the locust-swarm
Of fierce Mahrattas pillaging around
In the last century laid waste their land,
And left them subject to their suzerain
In name and truth. This, when the old blood stirs,
Is all forgotten like a vanished dream.
Too many chiefs the blight that nipped the flower
Of former greatness, manifest the seeds
Of weakness in the custom that divides
To every son his father's land in shares
Equal. Each country has its own fixed ways,

But by this Shekhawati surely forged
Her own subjection, tho' they say 'twas Fate.

That Sheikh Burhán should have a shrine, be held
In veneration, that his progeny
Is numerous and well dowered, is not strange.
But that these Rajputs carry reverence
So far that every man-child born to them
Wears for two years in infancy the garb,
Or emblem of the garb of Musalman,
And that they should abjure the flesh of hog,
Which other Rajputs love and hold it duty
To eat of once a year—is that not strange?

BUNDI

RAO RAJA SURJAN SINGH OF BUNDI AT BENARES

ABOUT A.D. 1586

I HEARD a voice last night when sleep refused
Its opiate, and it said reproachingly:
Rao Surjan, head of the brave Hara clan
Which sprang from the Chauhan who held Ajmere
And with it Ranthambor for centuries
Till the great fortress passed unto Méwar:
Rao Surjan, son of Arjan, who put on
The saffron at Chitor and glorified
The name of Bundi—his departure, bards
Have sung, the world amazed beheld. Rao Surjan

Holding in trust for Méwar Ranthambor

Betrayed his trust, bribed by the Emperor.

Sáwant the Hara and a virtuous few

Scorning to yield set up a pillar graved

With curse on Hara prince who should ascend

And quit the castle after with his life,

And then died fighting. From that day hath been

Silence between Méwar and Bundi: now

The Hara when he passes turns away

His face from Ranthambor lest he behold

A monument of shame. Was it for this

Rao Surjan bought the name Rao Raja?

Nay,

Just think—the Raja Mán Singh of Ambér,

When Akbar's army lay around below

The fortress, came to visit me attended

By a mace-bearer who, seen thro' disguise,

Was Akbar: straightway was a *gadi* laid,
Whereat the Emperor spake, and Raja Mán
Counselled surrender in return for gifts.
I thought of him my sire who at Chitor
Fell fighting—thought and spurned: again
The memory of Rana Ratna slaying
My ancestor his host by treachery
Came and I wavered: finally it seemed
I could ennoble Bundi and my clansmen
Most, the great Emperor being in my hands,
By wringing much advantage. Yes, I know
He promised government of territory
Large, but my heirs will reap the benefit
Of more than the Rao Raja then conferred.
I stipulated that no Bundi chief
Should give a princess to the Delhi throne;
Should pay the poll-tax, serve beyond the Indus;

That Bundi vassals should not be required
To send their wives or female relatives
At the *Naoroza* festival abhorred
To the imperial palace, and when summoned
Unto the hall of audience should enter
Armed at all points: their sacred edifices
Should be respected; service when exacted
Should place them under no Hindu commander:
Their horses should not bear the imperial brand;
That they should beat their kettle-drums in Delhi
As far as *Lal Darwaza*, the Red Gate,
And should not *kowtow* entering The Presence;
That Bundi should be evermore to Haras
Their capital, as Delhi to the Emperor.
Also he gave me residence at Kasi,[1]
With right of sanctuary in our holy city.
Were these not gifts to Bundi—lacking salt

To me perhaps who bought them by unfaith?
But have I not wiped out the evil from them?
Did I not win such victory for the King
That he, without petition, bade me take
Benares and Chunar and rule them well?
Have I not purged this district of dacoits
And banished thieves from villages and towns?
Have I not prayed and built and beautified?
Here in this city public edifices
Fourscore, and four-and-twenty baths besides
Proclaim my zeal; while my benevolence
Pilgrims from every quarter laud. 'Tis true,
'Tis true—but yet in spite of all these things
Would God it had been some one else not I
Who gave up Ranthambor![2] That deed hath cost
Much feed of Brahmans, yet it pricks me still.

[1] Benares. [2] See Note, p. 230.

THE DISCROWNING OF UMÉD SINGH[1]

A.D. 1771

My image upon the pyre
  Hath burned with the hair of my son,
And as tho' I had passed thro' the fire
  The twelve days mourning are done.
Thus Uméda the chief of the Haras
  Resigns what his sword had won.

Two hundred years, as ye know,
Have passed since Jahangir the King
At our greatness struck the first blow,
When he gave unto Madho Singh
Our Kotah, the pride of the Chambal,
By way of thank-offering.

For Haras divided he knew
Would never be strong: the old tree
Lost sap as her torn branches grew;
We fought our own kinsmen, and we
Had not only Moghal for suzerain
But Ambér for enemy.

Ye know how hard was his yoke ;
  My father in exile did die :
'Twas fourteen years ere I broke
  The usurper and forced him to fly.
Ah ! the price that I paid the Mahratta,
  It hath cost me many a sigh.

And still the thought of those years
  My bosom with anger fills :
Like a queen enslaved and in tears,
  Oppressed by a thousand ills,
Lay our Bundi, queen and a widow,
  Enthroned in her beautiful hills.

The tale of Hanja my steed,
  Whose statue stands in the square,
Ye know, and how in that need,
  Tho' I spoke the traitor fair,
My vassal of Indergarh rebelled
  And bade me depart elsewhere.

I was only a boy at the time,
  And when I recovered my own
Was content to forget his crime—
  Almost, till eight years had flown,
When the coward recalled it by throwing
  At the name of my sister a stone.

So the bride I offered Jeypore
  Was refused, and after I learned
His taunt was the seed of our war
  When the cocoa-nut was returned.
Then I vowed on the cur and his litter
  The vengeance methought he had earned.

I invited them, sire and son
  And grandson, to meet me one day,
And slaughtered them every one
  At a stroke. My friends, do you say
'Twas a treacherous act? Yea, I know it.
  For the soul of Uméda pray.

Fifteen years have I ruled
  Since the life of those men was shed :
The hot blood of youth hath cooled,
  And ye, O my people, have said
That I loved you, and Bundi hath prospered—
  Ah! but the thought of those dead,

The guilt of that deed, hath been
  My spectre and constant guest,
Hath come in the night between
  My head and the pillow it pressed ;
And therefore this present discrowning,
  I seek by penance for rest.

I retire to wash out that stain
In Gunga,[2] to search for increase
Of piety, if through much pain
The gods will have pity and cease
To torment me here and hereafter.
Farewell. Let my son rule in peace.

[1] See Note, pp. 231-34.
[2] The sacred river Ganges.

KOTAH AND JHÁLAWÁR

NEARLY three centuries and a half ago
  This land, once held by Bheels, then Bundi's fief,
  Was given by Shah Jahan to its first chief
Rao Madho Singh; and spite of many a blow

From warring kinsmen, siege from proud Ambér
  And the Mahratta, stoutly held its own.
  The bard still sings how Zalim saved the throne
When the brave Haras stood and fought in square

Close to Bhatwarra; and again ten years
  After that battle, when he turned aside
  The hordes of Holkar, spreading far and wide,
By skilful payment. Yet what groans and tears

Came through the hand that saved, and held in thrall
  For sixty years his sovereign and his race,
  Spread corn and wealth upon the country's face
To feed his power, protected her from all

Dominion save his own! Zalim, the bold,
  The handsome, famed for wisdom, wit,
  Soldier and statesman, matchless hypocrite,
Nestor of Rajasthán when blind and old—

The Jhála's pride and Hára's curse: whom Fate
After his death, to Hara's endless moan,
Bequeathed a kingdom [1] near his fort Gágrone,
Reft, as was Kotah, from the parent state.

[1] The treaty made by Kotah through Zalim Singh with the British Government provided that he and his heirs should retain the administration of the State under the Chief. This stipulation was cancelled in 1838, Jhalawar, a part of Kotah, being formed into a separate State, the Chief of which must be a descendant of Zalim Singh.

ZÁLIM SINGH

A.D. 1818

WHAT will they say of the Jhála, the young Foujdar who became
King of the country he served in all but the empty name,
Who bowed the pride of the Háras, was unequalled in Rajasthan?
Will they call him only a robber and class him with Amir Khan?

From the day I fought against Ambér and held the
Mahratta in fee
To the time when the British power spread over the land
like a sea
'Twas a soldier's fortune to hold what his sword had won
by guile,
The part of a statesman to meet his enemy's wile by wile.

The man who must see behind as well as in front, and
sleep
At night in an iron cage, why, his thoughts must needs
lie deep;
To trust in the faith of another is like pouring water on
sand:
How could I thus unravel the plots I have held in my
hand?

Cruel no doubt they will call me, the hot turmoil of
strife
Has made me value but lightly a Thakur's or peasant's
life;
Nay, my own have I risked as boldly—it is all a game
of chess,
Where the winner cares but little if the loser blame or
bless.

Would my star have mounted higher when I fought for
Oodeypore
Had the Rajput only driven the Mahratta from her
door?
But he broke us, I was wounded, a prisoner—all was
lost.
So I turned again to Kotah, to the Chief whom I had
crossed.

Crossed in love—well, he forgave me. I rose to power and fame,
To the terror of all moneyed men, who would not play my game.
For I eased them of their plunder: but ask the ryot now
Who made the land a cornfield and multiplied the plough?

Who, when other States were crumbling, kept this one safe and sound,
Had friends and spies in the councils of the Durbars all around—
When the cut-throat English soldiers were cursed by many a Court
Foresaw that tide of conquest, and steered this ship to port?

These eyes are blind to the sunlight, and face of friend and foe,
Eighty years have chilled and darkened the spirit's fire and glow,
But the old man's mind is steady, tho' thin and cold in his veins
The blood that careered at twenty like a river after the rains.

See, there is the English treaty, signed, sealed, beyond a doubt.
It gives me a written charter for all I had without,
And which I might have lost, the power and name of regent—nay,
It leaves to my heirs the regency for many a coming day.

Will they hold it? Only God knows. I kept my seat by
force,
And always said a Rajput's throne was on the back of his
horse.
But times are changing, after I am gone there will be
then
Some value in a sunnud from this new imperial pen.

All the Durbars of Rajwarra will now be coming in
To join the English redcoats, because they are strong
and will win:
They seek not to topple over thrones, or to look
behind
The rights of the men in power; they guarantee what
they find.

What with Moghal and Mahratta, two grindstones grinding small,
Rajasthan has swayed and tottered, like a man about to fall;
Every day a new marauder lifts his head and beats his drums;
Peace, with one strong arm protecting, will be welcome when it comes.

My son may see it, but often I think 'will he manage to guide this State?'
Well, I've done my best, and must leave the rest in the hand of inscrutable Fate.
One thing I know, I have ruled this land far better than any king:
And men will say the same some day who now curse Zalim Singh.

AT BHURTPORE

THE JÁTS[1]

Local guide loquitur.

THE Rajput's lineage veiled in cloud
May be of longer date than ours—
God knows what mysteries enshroud
The pedigrees of ruling powers.
Enough for us that Jats can çlaim
An ancient history and have made
Here and in Punjab such a name
That none of us need be afraid
To wear it, whether war or peace.
Whence came the Sikhs and Ranjit Singh?

Bhurtpore began to make increase
When Suraj Mal was chief and king.
He built this fort—how long ago?
A century and a half perchance:
'Tis not Chitor, with all the glow
Of ancient glory and romance;
Its fame is modern—ninety years
Or less since General Lake was here
And stormed in vain, tho' prudent fears
Led to surrender that same year.
Four months had Ranjit bravely held
These walls; the British loss was great;
But all their foes were being quelled,
And Ranjit wished to save his State.
Lord Lake was strong, had taken Deeg.
Holkar, who then was in this Fort
A refugee—with whom in league

We thought to cut the redcoats short—
Saw that the game was up : so peace
Was made and has remained, save when
Hot Durjan Sal by force took lease
Of fort and *gadi.* Then again
The redcoats came in Twenty-Six,
Stormed, and set up the rightful heir.
Bhurtpore has had no politics
Since then ; but fearful grief and care
Fell on us when the blood-red waves
Of mutiny in Fifty-Seven
Surged round and thro' and no one knew
Where next would work the deadly leaven.
Our chief a boy, those round him stood
Faithful to British salt and wise ;
This Fort the men of fire and blood
From Neemuch would have made their prize

But for the Durbar. Muttra near,
  Agra, the North-West, all in flame,
Had Rajasthan rebelled that year—
  Were all of us quite free from blame?
Ask Kotah—foolish men will be
  In every State; your records show
We let the lawless soldiery
  Go by and fought them too as foe.
Did we remember Najaf Khan
  A hundred years or so before,
And Sindhia later? Rajasthan
  Remembered, yet in such uproar
When men see blood and hear strange cries
  'Tis hard to sunder right from wrong,
Wisdom from folly's swift surprise.
  The British raj had lasted long
And was asleep, they said—not one

White soldier near :[2] the prophecy
That told the hundred years were done
Since Panipat when it should die
Had spread—thank God, we chose aright.
Now in Bhurtpore you may review
Troops kept for distant frontier fight.
Jodhpore and Jeypore, Ulwar too
And Bikanir, such troops maintain
Or transport. You should see our Chief
Move cavalry upon the plain.
He knows the drill-book, every leaf.[3]

[1] See Note, p. 234.

[2] See Note, p. 236.

[3] The Chief here referred to, Maharaja Jeswant Singh, G.C.S.I., died in December 1893.

ULWAR,[1] 1892

GARDENS and groves of orange, avenues
  Of shady trees; a city at the base
Of a steep rock-bound, fort-crowned hill; bright hues
  Of flowers and varied tillage; many a trace
Of Western thought in disciplined array
  Of troops, schools, hospitals; while all the East
Breathes in the palace of a bygone day,
  Which travellers praise and where they love to feast
Their eyes on pearls and books of ancient date
  And curious arms. These, with a fertile soil
And hardy race, are Ulwar—modern State,
  Twelve decades old; in ancient times the spoil

Of Moslem from the Rajput, till their creed
  Mixed with the Jadu's blood—a hybrid strain.
Báber and Akbar, Aurangzeb, thro' greed
  Of power came here and conquered : then again
The Ját from Bhurtpore raided fifty years ;
  Till the Narukas, sprung from Jeypore, seized
The helm which now their fifth chief calmly steers,
  Peace on the wave, and tumult all appeased.

[1] See Note, p. 236.

AMIR KHAN'S SOLILOQUY

AT TONK, A.D. 1818

THEY talk of their lineage old, these Chiefs of the Sun
and Moon,
And of me as a robber bold who founded a throne by
crime;
Let them hurl hard names as they please, my sons and
the world will soon
Forget how the robber rose; it is only a question of
time.

Their Rama and Krishna, methinks, if they ever existed,
were thieves,
Like Bappa and Jodha and all the strongest men who
have made
Kingdoms; the kingdoms of earth, what are they but
golden sheaves
To be bound by the men who have reaped, whose will
is to be obeyed?

Holkar and Sindhia were not so squeamish as these old
kings;
I served them well and they paid the labourer worthy
of hire.
Did I serve Jeypore when he paid? Did I break the
seal and strings
Of an oath when my guns spoke false as they raked
an ally with fire?

Jeypore perhaps may complain—that is one of my present griefs ;
Let it pass as an old mistake, and that of the same false guns
Which blundered the day at Nagore when forty of Marwar's chiefs,
Who came to feast at my tents as friends, made room for their sons.

Is there nothing more to regret? The cowards say that I slew
The girl they poisoned between them;[1] they laid her death at my door
Because I bullied the chief whose blood is bluest of blue
For a fee from that Raja Mán, the oily demon Rahtore.

Naught else? Nay, how should a man who held the
Rajput in thrall,
And who started in life with only the sword of a bold
Pathan,
Stickle at trifles to win, or even remember all
The blood that was shed as he fought in Malwa and
Rajasthan?

Why doth the brain that steeled break silence kept till
to-day
With thoughts like these of a womanish hue? I am
lord and king,
Have washed my hands and am clean from the blood and
smoke of the fray—
And shall I begin to fear the prick of a conscience-
sting?

Nay, 'tis only the whisper of things I fancy them saying
abroad
My brother chiefs—they will wince at that name; for
me 'tis enough
To have carved my way to a throne by the edge of a
fearless sword.
Conscience? A soldier like me is made of a sterner
stuff.

[1] See Rhyme on Krishna Kumari, page 53.

MISCELLANEOUS

LATEST ANECDOTE OF BIJEY SINGH OF MARWAR

The latest anecdote of Raja Bijey Singh of Marwar is contributed by the Jodhpore Administration Report for 1887-88, which says that he, "being himself a zealous Vishnav, strictly prohibited the manufacture and sale of liquor throughout the country, and that the prohibition remained in force in letter and spirit during a full period of twenty years. The Thakur of Ahwa, named Jét Singh, who had acted in opposition to these prohibitions, was seized and executed in the fort of Jodhpur on pretence of this very offence, though there existed a grudge against him on account of his unbearable insolence and defiance to the authority of the chief. The place, situated outside the 'Singoria Gate' of the city of Jodhpur, where the Thakur's corpse was burnt, is still worshipped by the Jodhpur *kalals* (liquor-sellers), who consider the Thakur as a hero and martyr who sacrificed his life for their cause."

COURTIERS

DIDST thou, O King, an edict frame and seal
That whoso brews or sells distillèd liquor
Shall straightway perish for his country's weal
To make and keep it sober all the quicker?

KING

'Tis true; and from that question I may guess
To loosen some one's head is now your notion,
Relying on the fact that I profess
To sect of Vishnu the most strict devotion.
Still I may pardon if need be, why not?
A case may call for reconsideration.

COURTIERS

The Ahwa Thakur is the culprit.

KING

What!
Jét Singh? This saves a lot of botheration.
The beast hath long authority defied—

COURTIERS

We thought the news would very likely please thee.

KING

My royal edict can't be set aside.
O holy Vishnu, thus do I appease thee!

Jét Singh is beheaded, and sainted as a martyr a hundred years after by the Jodhpur vintners, for whom the following elegy may serve :—

Thou wert murdered, brave Jét Singh,
By a water-drinking King :
Does he know that beef and beer
Brought the British soldier here ?
Whisky too he drinks no end,
Does the Englishman our friend,
Who our enemies did scatter,
Conquered Moghal and Mahratta.
Water never did nor can
Suit a Rajput nobleman :
Therefore, Thakur, didst thou die
In the cause of Liberty :
Liberty to tipple when
You like belongs to all free men.
" Rightly struggling to be free,"

Thee we praise, we honour thee.
Yes, to honour thee we come,
Martyr for our Indian rum,
Which the soldier in the barrack
Calleth by the name of arrack [1]
And to denizens of Maroo
Generally is known as *dharoo ;*
Ages long it has been made,
Hot and strong, it's good for trade ;
And if opium were not grown
We should each a fortune own.
So to worship thee we come,
Martyr for our Indian rum !

[1] *Araq,* essence.

THE ULWAR TRIAL

Kunj Behari Lal, a member of the Ulwur State Council, while driving in his carriage on a public road in Ulwur, on the 21st May 1892, was attacked by a party of men, and despatched by swords. The Maharaja having died suddenly at Naini Tal the day after, the inquiry into the murder was conducted by the British Government, with the result that four men were convicted by a court composed of two English officers lent to the State. The court found that the murder had been authorised by the Maharaja, and was planned by his right-hand man and staff-officer, Major Ram Chander, who, by means of pressure, had induced the others to accomplish it. Akhey Singh, who, with Ram Chander, was sentenced to death, openly confessed as to the part he and his associates had taken, instigated thereto by Ram Chander and believing the murder had been commanded by the Raj (Maharaja). The following lines reflect bazaar comment in Rajputana after the trial.

IF the Raj had only lived, father,

Where would have been the crime?

Most would have said, "Good riddance,

And not before it was time";

For the man had risen too fast, father,
  And had few friends in the place:
Alas, it was hard for the Raj to die,
  And leave this sad disgrace!

To kill on a public road, father,
  Was bad—the best men make
(As the ancient proverb hath it)
  At times, you know, a mistake.
Ram Chander lost his sense, father
  But it seems a terrible thing
For doing the Raj's own command
  To hang poor Akhey Singh.

And Buddha to *Kála Páni*[1]
  For life; seven years of jail
To Chandra the son of Chajju—
  Alas for the women who wail!

The dead man was not their rival
  Ram Chander's only—beside,
Just think, not one would have suffered
  If the Raj had never died!

You say the Sirkar[2] says, father,
  No Raj has power to kill,
But we know they have always done it,
  And some will do it still.

* * * * *

This case will make them fear, boy,
  And save some lives: our eyes
Are blind, our weak hearts tremble.
  The big Sirkar is wise.

[1] The common name for transportation across the sea or *black water*.

[2] The British Government is known as the Sirkar, and the Chief of a State as the Raj or the Durbar.

THE BAORI'S REQUEST

"Moghias (or Baoris) invariably select moonless nights for the commission of their crimes; and in this connection a native official lately informed me that he was present in Court when a Moghia was sentenced to a heavy fine, and actually heard the prisoner beg for permission that payment might be deferred until the nights grew dark!"—*Extract from Report of the Superintendent of Moghias in Rajputana and Central India for* 1893.

O FOR a land where the Baori
Has plenty to eat and to do!
Nowadays not a single *cowrie*
Can he raise without hullabaloo.
Time was that the Sétts when we raided
Were quick with the melting pot,
And the Raj and its Thakurs aided
If pursuit were getting hot.

It paid them well : and they fenced us
From harm in some ancient keep ;
But the Sirkar went against us,
And now it's little we reap.
There used to be lots for the scrambling
When a line of camels showed,
Or a fat Mahajan was ambling,
At night on a lonely road.

But the dear old days have departed,
The merry old times are gone ;
No wonder a chap's down-hearted
When he's always " downed upon."
These jails are enough to stifle
Men used to the jungle free ;
And it's hard to be fined for a trifle
That wasn't worth a rupee.

They have spoilt the taste and flavour
  Of life, these wretched police—
I ask your Honour a favour:
  If you let me go in peace
The fine shall be paid like rent, Sir,
  On the day it is due all right—
But I hope you will kindly consent, Sir,
  To wait till a moonless night.

STEPPING THE BOUNDARY

In days when laws and people
  Were primitive yet wise,
When villagers disputed
  O'er doubtful boundaries,
The Rajput and the Bheel alike
  Would choose a trusted man,
A grey-beard generally, who knew
  How every field began.

How here was waste till such an one
   Reclaimed it ; there a well,
Or watercourse, was made by A
   (His grandsire used to tell) ;
B sowed this land for twenty years ;
   That patch belonged to C :
The Grey-beard would be sure to know
   The boundary's history.

If only he would speak the truth,
   On which they trusted solely ;
For he would carry in his hand
   A little water holy,
And on his head a wild beast's skin,
   Or goat's, to show that he
If perjured of his oath a beast
   In the next world would be.

Thus fitted out, and solemnly
  Adjured by every god,
Before the assembled multitude
  The boundary he trod.
And where he stept the line was marked,
  And all men were content
To follow till the trace grew faint
  That boundary settlement.

Some churl perhaps when Grey-beard died,
  Some soured churl might say,
" A jackal that I heard last night
  Howling in search of prey
Reminded me of Grey-beard's voice :
  I always feared he'd rue
Thro' holy Gunga's wrath the day
  He cut my field in two."

But those who know the people well
Aver the country-side
Is thoroughly convinced and sure
That Grey-beard never lied:
And modern forms of settlement,
So seldom understood,
Are not, they think, as honest or
In fact one half as good.

Yet all agree the stepping mode
Is out of date, because
Of new inventions—railways, schools,
Piece-goods, vakeels and laws,
And fifty other things that since
It flourished have occurred—
To prove that as men "civilise"
You cannot trust their word.

A BHEEL DISPUTE

MÉWAR, 1891

The local manager advises

THE Bheels are out in Sigri—
  They're shouting in the name
Of Justice; and in Mádri
  The Bheels are all aflame.
For the Sigri men say Mádri
  Has cheated them of land:
A boundary dispute, you know,
  Is hard to understand.

And generally among the Bheels
  It leads to blood and riot.
This one both villages agreed
  To settle by panchayat:
Who took a man from each and made
  Them swear by gods divine,
Hand clasped in hand, impartially
  To step the boundary line.

And so they stept it. Sigri swears
  That sixty beegahs, sown
By them for twenty years, have now
  Been into Madri thrown:
Their man, they say, was small and weak,
  And Madri's big and strong;
The big man took the line he liked,
  And forced the weak along.

They also say the *panch*[1] was bad,
Or prejudiced, or bought,
And would not listen to their pleas
Or make the inquiry sought.
As far as I can judge, the tale
That Sigri tells is true,
But, true or false, the question is,
What is the Raj to do?

The Sahib has said both sides agreed
To arbitration—yes.
Therefore the *panch* must be upheld.
That's not so clear, I guess.
The Bheels are out, the *kilkie's*[2] raised
And therefore I'm afraid
The *status quo* must be restored
And fresh inquiry made.

[1] The usual abbreviaton of *panchayat*, a court of arbitration originally consisting of five (*pánch*) members.

[2] War-cry of the Bheels.

A PETITION

IN the restless days of yore, in
  The time my father was a lad,
Lony Ochter[1] Sahib came warring,
  Built the station Naseerbad;
Formed a regiment of Rasála
  At Rampura: with it came
Mahmood Khan from near Ambála—
  That, Sir, was my father's name.

You must know before their coming
  There had been a lot of trouble,
Half the country round was drumming
  Unto arms, and playing double.
Some were secretly inciting;
  But the brave Rasála showed
What Pathans can do in fighting.
  Through the district straight they rode.

Lony Ochter Sahib soon scattered
  All his enemies afar;
Mahmood Khan was wounded, battered,
  And promoted Rasaldar;
Given a jagír in this village,
  Which he founded, where I dwell,
Peaceably engaged in tillage,
  As my neighbours all can tell.

This, my son, is the Patwari,
He was taught by Ganesh Rám,
Who I'm quite sure would be sorry
If he came to any harm.
Yet this Moonserim [2] is trying
To withhold from us our due;
See, that field of mine is drying—
He won't let the water through.

What's the reason, sir? God knows it.
See, that channel from the tank—
I could open it or close it,
As the water rose and sank,
Give our village what it needed,
Store the rest; but now they say
Our supply must be impeded
For some land two miles away.

What would Mahmood Khan or Lony
  Ochter Sahib have said to this?
Ganesh Rám is widely known, he
  Is too straight to work amiss:
He forgets, though, that Rasála.
  What could such as he is know
Of Mahmood Khan from near Ambála,
  Him who made this village grow?

He is young—young men in work are
  Sharp and active: I am old.
What I say is, let the Sirkar
  Now the scales of justice hold.

*   *   *   *

So he spoke, with warmth yet wary,
  Weaving in and out his tale
Lony Ochter—Rasaldári
  As the words of most avail.

[1] Persons resident in the East do not require to be told that the common people have a curious way of speaking of Ochterlony as Lony Ochter.

[2] Moonserim, a sub-overseer in the Revenue Department.

SNAKE-BITE

AN INCIDENT OF MODERN AJMERE

THE woman Khori, the wife
  Of the herdsman Amar Singh,
Who saw her depart this life,
  And witnessed the cobra spring.
There wasn't a doubt of the fact
  From all that the neighbours said:
The snake was killed in the act
  And brought to the *thánah*[1] dead.

[1] A Police post, the head of which is called the *thánadár*.

But three weeks after a lad
Looked into a disused well:
And one month after a sad,
Sad story there was to tell.
The thánadár came and saw,
And (to cut the matter short)
Old Amar Singh and his brother-in-law
Confessed in the Sessions Court

They had put her out of the way
Because of her goings-on.
She went to the temple each day,
Tho' they told her not to. Upon
The temple steps she was seen
The night she was last alive.
And the priest he was young, with a full-fed spleen,
While Khori was forty-five.

And Rajput honour, you know,
    Recks little of English laws
In a case like that. Not a blow
    Was struck at the priest, because
All scandal they wished to hide.
    It was rather fine—was it not?
And hard that no family pride
    May now wipe out such a blot,

Without being chained like a thief,
    And banished across the seas.
There is the story in brief
    Of a snake-bite—which, if you please,
Is common enough. The tale
    In different forms you may learn
To read if you take up the trail
    Of many a snake-bite return.

A THAKUR AT HOME

(In a British District)

I

He lives amid a curious pile that towers
Above the mud-built dwellings of the herd,
Whose friend he is and chief of earthly powers.
The sorcerer's spell, the Brahman's blighting word
Maintain their sway beside his easy rule,
And no one seems to feel the Thakur's thrall,
For, save one modern thing, the Government School,
Time-honoured custom is the lord of all.

The sun goes down on droves of goats and kine
  Streaming within the village gates: the moon
Looks on the Thakur boosing o'er his wine
  And lulled by beat of drum in endless tune.
Contentment holds the village and its chief:
  The scene is one of dirt, but not of grief.

II

"A stagnant pool," the traveller may say:
  "A century breeds no change where grief and mind
Alike are not: none looks beyond to-day,
  Or knows the outer world; their joys are blind.
A man lies down beside the beast he drives,
  And eats his frugal meal without a sigh:
Is that the goal and end of human lives?—
  Content to live—content perhaps to die!"

Ah well! the outer world is pressing in
  And coming nearer to the stagnant pool,
And not to know will soon be held a sin—
  But is the Pundit happier than the fool?
God help the Thakur when he asks that question.
  It sticks a little in my own digestion.

A THAKUR IN A RAGE

(IN A NATIVE STATE)

FRIEND, do you say it is well for us that the big Sirkar
Is here to watch over our rights and our children's
rights in the land?
It seems to me to be more on the side of a proud Durbar
Which laughs secure at my wrong because I am tied
foot and hand.

Forty or fifty years ago this adoption case
 Would have cost my father no trouble; his castle was armed for fight,
His horses fleet, and his men the pick of an ancient race:
 A morning's ride and a dozen shots would have settled it all outright.

Now I must waste, it seems, a couple of years and more
 In a game of Vakils and pay a mongrel pleader to scrawl;
He says he is working my case, and has sent already a score
 Of petitions to Abu and Simla: I'm sick and tired of it all.

Scribes and judges may reap the rupees I have sown
broadcast,
But the Durbar will never forget it was weak when our
house was strong.
It seeks to lessen my power ; it owes me a grudge for the
past,
And is always watching and trying to make me out in
the wrong.

What do they want me to do? Go out on the jungle
side
With all my retainers and earn the name of an outlaw
bold?
If they force me ever to that, I will humble somebody's
pride ;
It shall cost them dear, my revenge—I will pay it a
thousandfold.

MAULED

At Siwai Madhopur (Jeypore)

3rd January 1893

One of an army of beaters,
    Five or six hundred men,
Followed a wounded tigress
    Down thro' a jungly glen ;
Saw her lying, and rashly,
    Foolishly, threw a stone—
(Says a shikari near him)
    We heard a roar and a groan.

Then four shots. The shikari
  (May bounce as shikaris can)
Says that he dropped the tigress
  Standing over the man.
Whatever the facts, his shooting
  Deserves a medal to win,
For he saved the life of the beater,
  Tho' he spoilt the tiger's skin.

Saved—let's hope: but a broken
  Arm from a tiger's jaws
And wounds upon head and body
  From those terrible fangs and claws
Must heal ere the reckless Naga
  Can be saved, poor fellow, outright,
And show with pride in his village
  The marks of a tiger's bite.

One of an army of beaters,
  Five or six hundred men,
Tracking a wounded tigress
  Down thro' a jungly glen—
Why have I told the story?
  Simply because he said,
" *Tell the Maharaja.*"

29th January

His name was
  Sheoram Dass—and he's dead:
The shikari's name has a Rajput ring,
  Shekhawat of Sikar is brave Oom Singh.

THE PRESENT SIEGE OF BHURTPORE

The Genius loci protests

THEY talk of the siege of Bhurtpore,
But never a thought they give,
As their guns they wipe, whether duck and snipe
Would rather die than live.

No place like this they declare,
And they call it sport and fun
As the fowl go by like clouds in the sky
To drop them one by one.

The white man's heart it is strong,
    We know his courage and pluck;
We are not Jain,[1] yet we cannot divine
    Why he shoots such myriads of duck.

'Tis good when a tiger dies,
    But we count it strange and harsh,
The passion some feel for duck and teal
    And snipe in the lonely marsh.

[1] The Jains object to the destruction of animal life in any shape, even of a noxious reptile or mad dog.

A SONG OF JODHPORE, 1893

THERE'S a place in Rajputana with a fort of old renown
And a liberal-hearted fine old king,
And the traveller who visits that most hospitable town
Hears a lot about Sir Pratap Singh.
He is Minister and Commandant of Cavalry in one,
And his fellows, by Jove, *can* ride ;
You should go there for a "pig-stick" if you want to see some fun :
There are pigs, Sir, on every side.

CHORUS

Hunting the gallant boar,
Englishman and Rahtore,
Brothers in sport, ride o'er
The sandy plain at Jodhpore.

They won the Polo Tournament this year, the plucky team
  Sir Pratap took to Poona t'other day;
And the liberal-hearted king, Maharaja Jeswant Singh,
  Says his men can fight as well as play;
We shall find them by our side if we ever have to ride
  On the frontier far away against the foe,
And we feel the brave Rahtore, like his ancestor of yore,
  Is an ally to be trusted, don't you know?

CHORUS

Hunting the gallant boar,
Englishman and Rahtore,
Brothers in sport, ride o'er
The sandy plain at Jodhpore.

Do we think too much of sport as good training for our
youth?
Is the teacher sick or sorry when his art
Makes his pupil better man than himself, do what he can?
Nay, he feels an honest pride in his heart.
For a victory o'er foe whose strength was never feared
Is nothing, and we keep the old rule,
Let all rivalry be keen and whoever wins be cheered—
That's the lesson we have learnt at school.

CHORUS

Hunting the gallant boar,
Englishman and Rahtore,
Brothers in sport, ride o'er
The sandy plain at Jodhpore.

FAMINE IN RAJPUTANA

1892

THE goddess of Chitor in olden time
  Craved regal victims—superstition tells:
  But this gaunt spectre ravages and dwells
Among the poor, in poverty and slime,
Tempting despair and maddening to crime.
  We read in former days how dried-up wells
  And barren fields brought death: old chronicles
Speak of slain hecatombs: but now like chime
Of bells o'er hills the railway's scream is heard.
  The Iron Horse has saved the land and scared

The spectre Famine, like some carrion bird
    Disturbed at its foul feast. Had God but spared
The poor man's cattle, ah, what joy had stirred
    The hearts of those for whom in need He cared!

THE HOUSE UPON THE LAKE

AJMERE, 19TH MARCH 1890

In varying mood four years and more
These eyes have seen the ripples break
And waves arise to wild wind's roar
Beside this house upon the lake.

Sunrise and sunset, and the play
Of light and shadow thro' the year—
I know them well, for night and day
The lake made music in mine ear.

The green in front, with birds and bloom
  And ferns and trees that shade the sky;
These marble walls, each quaint cool room—
  I leave them, not without a sigh,

To dwell upon a distant hill
  Already loved for its own sake:
But ah! to-day my thoughts are still
  With the old house upon the lake.

THE HOUSE UPON THE HILL

MOUNT ABU, 20TH MARCH 1894

FOUR years again have passed and schooled
Since mine the task with earnest will
To follow better men who ruled
From this bright house upon the hill.

The names of Lawrence, Sutherland,[1]
And others linger round its walls ;
Its garden fair a gentler hand,
O ferns and flowers, to me recalls.

Looking upon the lake below,
The hills around, beyond, I seem
To hear the sounds of Long Ago
As of those days I rhyme and dream.

'Tis classic ground, tho' railway near
May shriek ; I wonder, Abuji,
If ground there be not classic here
In Rajasthan so kind to me.

The Past and Present to compare,
From each its fragrance to distil,
Where could be fitter spot, O where,
Than this bright house upon the hill ?

[1] Lieutenant-Colonel J. Sutherland was Agent to the Governor-General for Rajputana from 1841 to 1848, and Sir Henry Lawrence from 1853 to 1857.

NOTES TO RHYMES

I VENTURE to preface these Notes with the following extract from the essay on the Rajput States in Sir Alfred Lyall's admirable book, *Asiatic Studies* (pp. 182-186):—

"The region to which we refer is that which is now called, in the administrative nomenclature of the Indian Empire, Rajputána; and, by the natives of India, Rajasthán, or the country of the chiefs. It is the region within which the pure-blooded Rajpút clans have maintained their independence under their own chieftains, and have in some instances kept together their primitive societies ever since the dominion of the Rajpúts over the great plains of North-Western India was cast down and broken to pieces seven centuries ago by the Musalmán irruptions from Central Asia. The first Musalmán invasions found Rajpút dynasties ruling in all the chief cities of the north and over the rich Gangetic plains eastward to the confines of modern Bengal—at Lahore, Delhi, Kanauj, and Ajodhya. Out of these great cities and fertile lands the Rajpút chiefs were driven forth southward and westward into the central regions of India, where a more difficult country gave them a second line of defence against the foreigners. And this line they have held not unsuccessfully up to the present day. The boundaries of their actual territory are not easily defined without a map, though no boundaries of political territory in India have varied so little in historic times. After the earliest Mahomedan conquests the Rajpút country seems to have extended (speaking roughly) from the Indus and the Sutlej on the west and north-west right across the Indian continent eastward up to the vicinity of the Jumna River at Agra and Delhi, and southward until it touched the Vindhya range of mountains. This great central region had for its natural barriers on the west and north-west the desert, on the east the rocky, broken tracts which run along west of the Jumna, and on the south the passes and woodlands of the Vindhya mountains. And though in many parts of this country, to the south and south-east especially, the dominion of the Rajpúts has been overlaid by Mahomedan or Maratha usurpations, yet everywhere Rajpút septs or petty chiefships may still be found existing in various degrees of independence. And there are, of course, Rajpút chiefs outside Rajputána altogether, though none of political importance. But Rajputána proper, the country still under the independent rule of the most ancient families of the purest clans, may now be understood generally to mean the great tract that would be crossed by two lines, of which one should be drawn on the map of India from the frontier of Sind eastward to the gates of Agra; and the other from the southern border of the Punjab Government near the Sutlej southward and south-eastward until it meets the broad belt of Maratha States under the Guicowar, Holkar, and Sindia, which runs across India from Baroda to Gwalior. This territory is divided into nineteen states, of which sixteen are possessed by Rajpút clans, and the chief of the clan or sept is the state's ruler. To the Sesodia clan, the oldest and purest blood in India, belong the States of Oodipoor, Banswarra, Pertábgarh, and Shahpura; to the Rathore clan, the States of Jodhpoor and Bikanír; Jeypoor and Ulwar to the Kuchwáha; and so on.

"Of these states the highest in rank and the most important politically are the States of Oodipoor, Jodhpoor, and Jeypoor. The ancestors of the family which now rules in Oodipoor were hereditary leaders of the clan which has held from time immemorial, from a date before the earliest Mahomedan invasion, the country which now forms the territory of their chief; the chiefs of Jodhpoor and Jeypoor are the descendants of families who gave princes to the tribes that were dominant in Upper India before the Musalmáns came. In fact, all these states have very much the same territorial origin; they are the lands which a clan, or a sept, or a family, has seized and settled upon, and have managed to hold fast through centuries of warfare. And what we know of the manner in which these states were founded gives a very fair sample of the movements and changes of the primitive world. When the dominant Rajpút families lost their dominion in the rich Gangetic plains, one part of their clan seems to have remained in the conquered country, having submitted to the foreigner, cultivating in strong communities of villages and federations of villages, and paying such land-tax as the ruler could extract. These communities still exist and flourish in British India, where there are very many more Rajpúts than in Rajputána. Another part of the clan, probably the near kinsmen of the defeated chief, followed his family into exile, and helped him to carve out another, but a much poorer, dominion. They discovered a tract just productive enough to yield them food, and wild enough to shelter them from the great armies of the foreigner. Here the chief built himself a fort upon a hill; his clansmen slew or subdued the tribes they found in possession of the soil, and the lands were all parcelled off among the chief's kinsfolk, the indigenous proprietors being subjected to payment of a land-tax, but not otherwise degraded. Having thus made a settlement and a city of refuge, the chief and his Rajpúts started upon an interminable career of feuds and forays, striving eternally to enlarge their borders at the cost of their neighbours. When the land grew too strait for the support of the chief's family or of the sept—that is, when there were no vacant allotments—a landless son of the chief would assemble a band and set forth to make room for himself elsewhere. If he was lucky, he found his room; if not, the family was rid of his company: in either event he was provided for. In this way the whole country of Rajputána was occupied by the clans and septs which we now find there; and their territories are now called by us states; but these states are constitutionally quite unlike any others in India. For, while everything else in the political order of India has changed, the Rajpút States have managed to preserve unaltered much of their original structure, built up out of the needs and circumstances of primitive life. The strain of incessant warfare, in which these tribal sovereignties were engaged from their foundation centuries ago until the English peace of 1818, has served to keep tight the bonds which held them together, without being violent enough to break them asunder. Of course the original type has undergone some modifications; towns have grown up round the ancient forts; the lands of each sept have gradually, and by constant friction, rounded themselves off into distinct territories; and the chiefs have in some instances succeeded in modernising their status toward the likeness of territorial sovereignty. But on the whole there are probably few or no political fabrics having any pretence to be called states, in any part of historic Asia, which have suffered so little essential change between the eleventh and nineteenth centuries—a period which for Rajputána was one long war-time, from the first inroads of the Ghaznevi kings to the final pacification of Central India by the military and political measures of the English Governor-General, Lord Hastings.

"During these seven centuries or so the Rajpút clans had various fortunes. The kings of the early Musalmán dynasties in Northern India pierced their country from end to end by rapid rushing invasions, plundering and ravishing, breaking the idols, and razing the beautifully-sculptured temples, Buddhist and Brahmanic. But so long as the object of these incursions was mere booty or fanatical slaughter, there was not much to be got out of the interior of Rajputána. The chiefs retired to their fortresses, great circumvallations of the broad tops of scarped hills, with three or four lines of defence, strongholds which cost the enemy a siege of some twelve or eighteen months, with the grand finale of a desperate sally *en masse* upon your lines by the garrison without hope or fear, dressed in saffron garments, drunk with opium and with the blood of their own womankind. The victor in obstinate and dangerous conflicts of this kind found himself paying rather dear for a warlike triumph; and as for conquest in the sense of establishing permanent dominion, the country was not worth the trouble of holding it against the clans and their faithful allies, the aboriginal non-Aryan tribes of the jungle. So early as the end of the twelfth century, nevertheless, the Mahomedans had discovered the great importance, as a *point d'appui* in the middle of the Rajpút country, of Ajmere, a city lying at the foot of an almost impregnable hill fort, well watered for these arid tracts, in a situation at once strong, central, and most picturesque. The fort was taken by the Afghan King Shaháb-ud-din at the end of the twelfth century; and on the crest of the hill the traveller is still shown a grave-yard thick with mounds, where are said to lie the bones of the faithful Islamites who fell in the storm, or in the massacre by which the Rajpúts celebrated the fort's recapture a few years later. Since then Ajmere has been lost and won several times; its possession being the symbol of political predominance in Rajputána: for it is a Castle Dangerous which no government could hold in the midst of the clans without powerful supports and the prestige of military superiority. The Moghal Emperors made it an imperial residence in the seventeenth century; in the confusion of the eighteenth century the Rajpúts got it again for a while, but soon had to yield it to the Maratha chief Sindia, then at the height of his fortunes. By him it was ceded, with the lands adjoining, to the British in 1818; and thus for six centuries or more, with a few intervals, Ajmere has contained the garrison by which the masters of India have enforced their paramount jurisdiction over the unruly clans of Rajputána."

THE MEWAR FAMILY. P. 25

The following extract from a sketch of Chitor compiled from Tod and other authorities by Dr. Stratton, resident at Oodeypore a few years ago, relates to the Mewar family:—

"In the beginning of the eighth century Chitor was the seat of the Mori division of the Pramar or Puar Rajputs then ruling in Mewar and Malwa; but it was taken about A.D. 728 by Bashpa, usually called Bappa, the ancestor of the present Maharana, since which time it has, with brief interruption arising from the fortunes of war, continued with the present house. But Chitor and the rich plains of Mewar were not the first possessions of this dynasty on the central plateau of India. For nearly two centuries previously it had ruled in Bhilwar, the wild hill country of the Bhils, which buttresses that plateau on the west, between Idar on the south and modern Udaipur on the north. Prior to that again it had for nearly four centuries held sway in the western peninsula of Saurashtra, now called Kathiawar. The vicissitudes of the family already alluded to were illustrated alike in its coming to the Bhil highlands and the Mewar plains, if not also in its earlier migration to the sea-coast province on the west. These stages and their epochs in the course of the Suryabans Rajputs, successively settling in Saurashtra, Bhilwar, and finally in Mewar, are historical, though the details of such remote periods are legendary."

TRANSLATION OF A GRANT OF LAND HELD BY A BRAHMAN. P. 26

"GRANT HELD BY A BRAHMIN OF BIRKHAIRAH.

"A Brahmin's orphan was compelled by hunger to seek sustenance in driving an oil-mill; instead of oil the receptacle was filled with blood. The frightened oilman demanded of the child who he was; 'A Brahmin's orphan,' was the reply. Alarmed at the enormity of his guilt in thus employing the son of a priest, *he covered the palm of his hand with earth, in which he sowed the tulsai seed*, and went on a pilgrimage to Dwarica. He demanded the presence (*dursuna*) of the god; the priests pointed to the ocean, when he plunged in and had an interview with Dwarica Nath, who presented him with a written order on the Rana for forty-five *bigahs* of land. He returned and threw the writing before the Rana, on the steps of the temple of Juggernat'h. The Rana read the writing of the god, placed it on his head, and immediately made out the grant. This is three hundred and fifty years ago, as recorded by an inscription on stone, and his descendant Koshala yet enjoys it."—(A true translation.—J. TOD.) Tod, vol. i. p. 552.

THE JOHUR. P. 35

In his *Annals of Mewar* Tod refers to several instances when a whole tribe has been extinguished by this awful rite, and observes as follows :—

"To the fair of other lands the fate of the Rajpootni must appear one of appalling hardship. In each stage of life death is ready to claim her: by the poppy at its dawn, by the flames in riper years; while the safety of the interval depending on the uncertainty of war, at no period is her existence worth a twelvemonth's purchase. The loss of a battle, or the capture of a city, is a signal to avoid captivity and its horrors, which to the Rajpootni are worse than death. To the doctrines of Christianity Europe owes the boon of protection to the helpless and the fair, who are comparatively safe amidst the vicissitudes of war; to which security the chivalry of the Middle Ages doubtless contributed. But it is singular that a nation so refined, so scrupulous in its ideas with regard to females, as the Rajpoot, should not have entered into some national compact to abandon such proof of success as the bondage[1] of the sex. We can enter into the feeling and applaud the deed which ensured the preservation of their honour by the fatal *Johur* when the foe was the brutalised Tatar. But the practice was common in the international wars of the Rajpoots; and I possess numerous inscriptions (on stone and on brass) which record as the first token of victory the captive wives of the foeman. When 'the mother of Sisera looked out of the window, and cried *through the lattice*, Why tarry the wheels of his chariot?—have they not sped? have they not divided the prey, to every man a damsel or two?' we have a perfect picture of the Rajpoot mother expecting her son from the foray.

---

[1] *Bunda* is "a bondsman" in Persia; *bandi*, "a female slave" in Hindi.

"The Jewish law with regard to female captives was perfectly analogous to that of Menu; both declare them 'lawful prize,' and both Moses and Menu establish rules sanctioning the marriage of such captives with the captors. 'When a girl is made captive by her lover, after a victory over her kinsman,' marriage 'is permissible by law.'[1] That forcible marriage, in the Hindu law termed *rachasa*, viz. 'the seizure of a maiden by force from her house while she weeps and calls for assistance, after her kinsman and friends have been slain in battle,'[2] is the counterpart of the ordinance regarding the usage of a captive in the Pentateuch,[3] excepting the '*shaving of the head*,' which is the sign of complete slavery with the Hindu. When Hector, anticipating his fall, predicts the fate which awaits Andromache, he draws a forcible picture of the misery of the Rajpoot; but the latter, instead of a lachrymose and enervating harangue as he prepared for the battle with the same chance of defeat, would have spared her the pain of plying the 'Argive loom' by her death. To prevent such degradation, the brave Rajpoot has recourse to the *Johur*, or immolation of every female of the family: nor can we doubt that, educated as are the females of that country, they gladly embrace such a refuge from pollution. Who would not be a Rajpoot in such

---

1 Menu, *On Marriage*, art. 26.

2 Menu, *On Marriage*, art. 33.

3 "When thou goest forth to war against thine enemies, and the Lord thy God hath delivered them into thine hands, and thou hast taken them captive, and seest among the captives a beautiful woman, and hast a desire unto her, that thou wouldest have her to thy wife; then thou shalt bring her home to thine house; and she shall shave her head, and pare her nails; and she shall put the raiment of her captivity from off her, and shall remain in thine house, and bewail her father and her mother a full month: and after that thou shalt go in unto her, and be her husband, and she shall be thy wife."—Deut. chap. xxi. vv. 10-13.

a case? The very term widow (*rand*) is used in common parlance as one of reproach.

"Menu commands that whoever accosts a woman shall do so by the title of 'sister,'[1] and that 'way must be made for her, even as for the aged, for a priest, a prince, or a bridegroom'; and in the admirable text on the laws of hospitality he ordains that 'pregnant women, brides, and damsels shall have food[2] before all the other guests'; which, with various other texts, appears to indicate a time when women were less than now objects of restraint—a custom attributable to the paramount dominion of the Mohamedans, from whose rigid system the Hindus have borrowed. But so many conflicting texts are to be found in the pages of Menu, that we may pronounce the compilation never to have been the work of the same legislator: from whose dicta we may select with equal facility texts tending to degrade as to exalt the sex. For the following he would meet with many plaudits: 'Let women be constantly supplied with ornaments at festivals and jubilees, for if the wife be not elegantly attired, she will not exhilarate her husband.' A wife gaily adorned, 'the whole house is embellished.'[3] In the following text he pays an unequivocal compliment to her power: 'A female is able to draw from the right path in this life, not a fool only, but even a sage, and can lead him in subjection to desire or to wrath.' With this acknowledgment from the very fountain of authority, we have some ground for asserting that 'les femmes font les mœurs,' even in Rajpootana; and that though immured and invisible, their influence on society is not less certain than if they moved in the glare of open day.

---

[1] *Cn Education*, art. 129.
[2] *On Marriage*, art. 114.
[3] *On Marriage*, arts. 57, 60-63.

"Most erroneous ideas have been formed of the Hindu female from the pictures drawn by those who never left the banks of the Ganges. They are represented as degraded beings, and that not one in many thousands can even read. I would ask such travellers whether they know the name of Rajpoot, for there are few of the lowest chieftains whose daughters are not instructed both to read and write; though, the customs of the country requiring much form in epistolary writing, only the signature is made to letters. But of their intellect, and knowledge of mankind, whoever has had to converse with a Rajpootni guardian of her son's rights must draw a very different conclusion. Though excluded by the Salic Law of India from governing, they are declared to be fit regents during minority; and the history of India is filled with anecdotes of able and valiant females in this capacity."

RÁKHI BHAI. P. 40

In his *Annals of Mewar* Tod writes :—

"Buhadoor had remained but a fortnight, when the tardy advance of Hemayoon with his succours warned him to retire. According to the annals, he left Bengal at the solicitation of the queen Kurnavati; but instead of following up the spoil-encumbered foe, he commenced a pedantic war of words with Buhadoor, punning on the word 'Cheetore.' Had Hemayoon not been so distant, this catastrophe would have been averted, for he was bound by the laws of chivalry, the claims of which he had acknowledged, to defend the queen's cause, whose knight he had become. The relation of the peculiarity of a custom analogous to the taste of the chivalrous age of Europe may amuse. When her Amazonian sister the Rahtore queen was slain, the mother of the infant prince took a surer method to shield him in demanding the fulfilment of the pledge given by Hemayoon when she sent the *Rákhi* to that monarch.

"'The festival of the bracelet' (*Rákhi*) is in spring, and whatever its origin, it is one of the few when an intercourse of gallantry of the most delicate nature is established between the fair sex and the cavaliers of Rajast'han. Though the bracelet may be sent by maidens, it is only on occasions of urgent necessity or danger. The Rajpoot dame bestows with the Rakhi the title of adopted brother; and while its acceptance secures to her all the protection of a '*cavaliere serviente*,' scandal itself never suggests any other tie to his devotion. He may hazard his life in her cause, and yet never receive a smile in reward, for he cannot even see the fair object who, as brother of her adoption, has constituted him her defender. But there is a charm in the mystery of such connexion, never endangered by close observation, and the loyal to the fair may well attach a value to the public recognition of being the *Rákhi-bund Bháe*, the 'bracelet-bound brother' of a princess. The intrinsic value of such pledge is never looked to, nor is it requisite it should be costly, though it varies with the means and rank of the donor, and may be of flock silk and spangles, or gold chains and gems. The acceptance of the pledge and its return is by the *katchli*, or corset, of simple silk or satin, or gold brocade and pearls. In shape or application there is nothing similar in Europe; and as defending the most delicate part of the structure of the fair, it is peculiarly appropriate as an emblem of devotion. A whole province has often accompanied the *katchli*, and the monarch of India was so pleased with this courteous delicacy in the customs of Rajast'han, on receiving the bracelet of the princess Kurnavati, which invested him with the title of her brother, and uncle and protector to her infant Oody Sing, that he pledged himself to her service, 'even if the demand were the castle of Rinthumbor.' Hemayoon proved himself a true knight, and even abandoned his conquests in Bengal when called on to redeem his pledge, and succour Cheetore, and the widows and minor sons of Sanga Rana.[1] Hemayoon had the highest proofs of the worth of those courting his protection; he was with his father Baber in all his wars in India, and at the battle of Biana his prowess was conspicuous, and is recorded by Baber's own pen. He amply fulfilled his pledge, expelled the foe from Cheetore, took Mandoo by assault, and, as some revenge for her king's aiding the king of Guzzerat, he sent for the Rana Bikramajeet, whom, following their own notions of investiture, he girt with a sword in the captured citadel of his foe."

"*THE WRATH OF THAT DREAD GODDESS WHO AYE CRAVED PRINCES FOR VICTIMS.*" P. 44

The following is taken from Stratton's sketch of Chitor, referred to in a previous note :—

"Superstition had it that when the fortress was in danger the goddess

[1] "Many romantic tales are founded on 'the gift of the Rakhi.' The author, who was placed in the enviable situation of being able to do good, and on the most extensive scale, was the means of restoring many of these ancient families from degradation to affluence. The greatest reward he could, and the only one he would, receive, was the courteous civility displayed in many of these interesting customs. He was the '*Rakhi-bund Bhae*' of, and received 'the bracelet' from, three queens of Oodipoor, Boondi, and Kotah, besides Chund-Bae, the maiden sister of the Rana; as well as many ladies of the chieftains of rank, with whom he interchanged letters. The sole articles of 'barbaric pearl and gold' which he conveyed from a country where he was six years supreme are these testimonies of friendly regard. Intrinsically of no great value, they were presented and accepted in the ancient spirit, and he retains them with a sentiment the more powerful because he can no longer render them any service."—Tod, vol. i. p. 313.

of Chitor always required the sacrifice of a crowned head in its defence. Twelve had perished on the first occasion, and on the second, though the Rana himself had not, the Prince of Deolia (Pertabgarh), a branch of the Chitor house, was killed with the ensign of Mewar waving over him. It was an evil omen, therefore, when, during this third siege, Udai Sing departed from Chitor, though there was no lack of chieftains of Mewar and allies from elsewhere, including the Tuar Prince of Gwalior, who failed not in its defence; as with the Sisodias and many of the related tribes of Rajputs, Chitor was considered as much a sanctuary of the Hindu religion as a fortress of Hindu power.

"The Rao of Salumbar was killed at the Surajpol, *i.e.* the Gate of the Sun, on the eastern brow. Indeed, the list of chiefs who fought and fell would be one of all the highest nobles of Mewar, and of many from neighbouring territories. But the two whose names have been remembered most, and were singularly immortalised by Akbar himself, were Patta Sing of Kailwa, a Sisodia of the Salumbar branch, and Jai Mal Rahtor of Bednor. When the Rao of Salumbar fell and the father of Patta Sing was also slain, important command devolved on the latter, then merely a lad of sixteen and lately married. His widowed mother thought she could do her country better service by dying in fight than resigning herself in *sati.* So making Patta put on clothes of saffron colour to mark his resolve, she armed herself, and in order that there might be no looking back on the part of her son for his young bride left behind, she armed her too with a lance, and the three—Patta Sing, his mother, and his girl-wife—descended the hill, and all fell fighting at its foot.

"With such example before them, the garrison had no thought of surrender; but when, after a lengthened siege, the northern defences had been destroyed, the garrison weakened by famine, and Jai Mal of Bednor, the commander, had been wounded, no means remained of longer resistance. The wounding of Jai Mal is thus described. He was on the battlements at night directing repairs, when Akbar, said to have been accompanied by the Jaipur chief, was moving through the advanced lines of his camp. Seeing a light on the fort wall he fired his favourite matchlock. Next day it was known the ball, "shot at a venture" in the night, had wounded Jai Mal; and Mussulman records state that Akbar, who previously called his matchlock 'durust andaz,' or the straight-thrower, thereon dubbed it 'Singram,' as meriting now the name of a hero. Jai Mal, scorning to die by a distant shot, was, in the next attempt of the garrison to drive back the enemy, carried out on the shoulders of a stalwart clansman, and so was killed fighting as he wished. All, however, was of no avail, and again the fearful closing scenes of the two earlier sieges were repeated, the ladies and women in thousands being sacrificed; the men then going out to their last fight, and the conqueror coming in. Whether Akbar was irritated at the prolonged defence or his troops were out of hand, it is said that the work of subsequent slaughter and demolition was even greater and more deliberate on this than on the two former occasions. Yet he marked his appreciation of the valour of Jai Mal and Patta in a singular way—by having effigies of them carved in stone, which he placed on stone elephants at the gateway of his palace at Delhi. There they were seen and described a century later by the traveller Bernier in A.D. 1563; but subsequently they were removed by Aurangzeb as savouring of image-making. Some time ago they were discovered, and are now to be seen at Delhi, not the least interesting of the archæological remains there, though whether they were meant by Akbar in honour of his Rajput opponents, or of himself as the conqueror of such men, is a doubtful point.

"With this, the last of the three great sacks by the Mussulmans, the stirring story of old Chitor may be said to close. Though recovered in Jahangir's time by Rana Amra Sing, grandson of Udai Sing, from an uncle of the latter, in whose hands the Emperor had found it politic to place it, and though always held the chief fortress of Mewar, it was not thereafter maintained by the Ranas as their capital of residence, its buildings were left unrepaired, and its subsequent history, which has been comparatively uneventful, may be summed up in the word—decay—as can be read also in its crumbling ruins."

The condition of Chitor in the time of Akbar's successor was thus noticed by the ambassador, Sir Thomas Roe, who passed it on his way up country in 1615:—

* * * * * *

* * "Cytor, an ancient citie ruined on a hill, but so that it appears a tomb of wonderful magnificence. There stands upon above one hundred churches, all of carved stone, many faire towers and landthornes cut throw many pillars, and innumerable houses, but no one inhabitant. There is but one ascent to the hill, it being precipitous, sloaping up, cut out of the rock, having four gates in the ascent before one arrive at the citie gate, which is magnificent. The citie is incompassed at the top about eight course, and at the south-west end a goodly old castle. I lodged by a poor village at the foot of the hill. This citie stands in the country of one Ranna, a Prince newly subdued by this King, or rather brought to confesse tribute. This citie was wonne by Ecbarsha, father to this Mogoll."

The ambassador's chaplain, the Rev. Edward Terry, similarly described it:—

"Chitor, an antient great kingdome, the chief citie so called, which standeth on a mighty high hill flat on the top, walled about at the least ten

English miles. There appear to this day above an hundred ruin'd churches and divers fair palaces, which are lodged in like manner among their ruins, besides many exquisite pillars of carved stone, and the ruins likewise of an hundred thousand stone houses. . . . It was won from Ranas, an antient Indian Prince, who was forced to live himself ever after in high mountainous places adjoining to that province, and his posterity to live there ever since. Taken from him it was by Achabar Padsha (the father of that King who lived and reigned when I was in those parts) after a very long siege which famished the besieged, without which it could never have been gotten."

It may be noted that Jai Mal's descendants are still strong at Bednor, and those of Patta Sing at Amet.

"*DOOMED HER OWN CHILD.*" P. 44

"Oody Sing was about six years of age. He had gone to sleep after his rice and milk, when his nurse was alarmed by screams from the *rawula*,[1] and the Bari,[2] coming in to take away the remains of the dinner, informed her of the cause, the assassination of the Rana. Aware that one murder was the precursor of another, the faithful nurse put her charge into a fruit basket, and covering it with leaves she delivered it to the Bari, enjoining him to escape with it from the fort. Scarcely had she time to substitute her own infant in the room of the prince, when Bunbeer, entering, inquired for him. Her lips refused their office; she pointed to the cradle, and beheld the murderous steel buried in the heart of her babe. The little victim to fidelity was burnt amidst the tears of the *rawula*, the inconsolable household of their late

[1] The seraglio, or female palace.

[2] Bari, Naé, are names for the barbers, who are the *cuisiniers* of the Rajpoots.

sovereign, who supposed that their grief was given to the last pledge of the illustrious Sanga. The nurse (Dhaé) was a Rajpootnee of the Kheechee tribe, her name Punna, or 'the Diamond.' Having consecrated with her tears the ashes of her child, she hastened after that she had preserved. But well had it been for Mewar had the poniard fulfilled its intention, and had the annals never recorded the name of Oody Sing in the catalogue of her princes."—Tod's *Annals of Mewar.*

THE RANA KARAN. P. 47

Rana Karan, A.D. 1621, was the first chief who waited on the Emperor (Jahangir), the independence of Mewar having departed with his father Amra. Jagat Singh succeeded A.D. 1628.

"*AMBER AND MARWAR ONCE MORE AT OUR SIDE.*" P. 48

"The princes of Amber and Marwar repaired to Rana Umra at Oodipoor, where a triple league was formed, which once more united them to the head of their nation. This treaty of unity of interests against the common foe was solemnised by nuptial engagements, from which those princes had been excluded since the reigns of Akber and Pertáp. To be readmitted to this honour was the basis of this triple alliance, in which they ratified on oath the renunciation of all connexion, domestic or political, with the empire. It was moreover stipulated that the sons of such marriage should be heirs, or if the issue were females, that they should never be dishonoured by being married to a Mogul.

"But this remedy, as will be seen, originated a worse disease; it was a sacrifice of the rights of primogeniture (clung to by the Rajpoots with extreme pertinacity), productive of the most injurious effects, which introduced domestic strife, and called upon the stage an umpire not less baneful than the power from whose iron grasp they were on the point of freeing themselves: for although this treaty laid prostrate the throne of Baber, it ultimately introduced the Mahrattas as partisans in their family disputes, who made the bone of contention their own."—Tod, vol. i. p. 399.

TRANSLATION OF THE GRANT FOR NATHDWARA. P. 58

"Sri Mahrana Bhima Sing-ji, commanding.

"To the towns of Sri-ji, or to the (personal) lands of the *Gosaén-ji*,[1] no molestation shall be offered. No warrants or exactions shall be issued or levied upon them. All complaints, suits, or matters, in which justice is required, originating in Nat'hdwara, shall be settled there; none shall interfere therein, and the decisions of the Gosaén-ji I shall invariably confirm. The town and transit duties[2] (of Nat'hdwara and villages pertaining thereto), the assay (*purkhaye*)[2] fees from the public markets, duties on precious metals (*kasoti*),[2] all brokerage (*dulali*), and dues collected at the four gates; all contributions and taxes of whatever kind, are presented as an offering to Sri-ji; let the income thereof be placed in Sri-ji's coffers.

"All the products of foreign countries imported by the Vaishnuvas,[3] whether domestic or foreign, and intended for consumption at Nat'hdwara,[4]

---

[1] The high-priest.

[2] All these are royalties, and the Rana was much blamed, eve[illegible] s Vishnuva ministers, for sacrificing them even to Kaniya.

[3] Followers of Vishnu, Crishna, or Kaniya, chiefly mercantile.

[4] Many merchants, by the connivance of the conductors of the cara[illegible] Nat'h-ji's goods, contrived to smuggle their goods to Nat'hdwara, and, [illegible]

shall be exempt from duties. The right of sanctuary (*sirna*) of Sri-ji, both in the town and in all his other villages,[1] will be maintained: the Almighty will take cognisance of any innovation. Wherefore, let all chiefs, farmers of duties, beware of molesting the goods of Nat'h-ji (the god), and wherever such may halt, let guards be provided for their security, and let each chief convey them through his bounds in safety. If of my blood, or if my servants, this warrant will be obeyed for ever and for ever. Whoever resumes this grant will be a caterpillar in hell during 60,000 years.

"By command—through the chief butler (*panairi*) Eklingdas: written by Surut Sing, son of Nat'hji Pancholi, Mah-sud 1st, Samvat 1865; A.D. 1809."
—From Tod's *Annals of Mewar*.

THE RAHTORES. P. 59

Seoji, 1212 A.D. Jodha founded Jodhpur 1489 A.D. Bika, sixth son of Jodha, founded Bikanir after Jodha Ganga A.D. 1516.

In his time Marwar united with Mewar to oppose Moghal invasion under Baber, but were defeated in the fatal field of Biana by treachery.

Maldeo succeeded Ganga A.D. 1532, and so employed his power against friend and foe that he became the first prince in Rajwarra, or, in the words of Ferishta, "the most potent prince in Hindustan." He redeemed the two most

---

disgrace of the high-priest or his underlings, this traffic was sold for their personal advantage. It was a delicate thing to search these caravans, or to prevent the loss to the state from the evasion of the duties. The Rana durst not interfere lest he might incur the penalty of his own anathemas. The author's influence with the high-priest put a stop to this.

[1] This extent of sanctuary is an innovation of the present Rana's, with many others equally unwise.

important possessions of his house, Nagore and Ajmere, and among other conquests dispossessed the sons of Bika of supreme power in Bikanir, captured and restored Serohi from the Deoras, from which house was his mother. Akbar, born at Umerkote during the flight of Humayoon, invaded Marwar A.D. 1561, and established Bikanir in independence of the parent state Jodhpur. Maldeo died A.D. 1569, and at his death "the banner of the empire floated pre-eminent over the *panch ranga*, the five-coloured flag which had led the Rahtores from victory to victory and waved from the sandhills of Umerkote to the salt lake of Sambhur." Oodey Singh, his son, gave a daughter in marriage to Akbar, who conferred on him the title of Raja and used to call him the "King of the Desert" and "Oodey the Fat." He restored to Oodey Singh all the possessions he had wrested from Marwar except Ajmere.

Soor Singh succeeded his father Oodey Singh A.D. 1595, and died in the Deccan A.D. 1620. He was succeeded by Guj Singh, who died A.D. 1638. Then came Jeswant Singh, who ruled forty-two years, dying at Kabul A.D. 1681. In the struggle for empire among the sons of Shah Jahan he fought for Prince Dara, who nominated him Viceroy of Malwa. Kishen, ninth son of Oodey Singh, founded Kishengurh A.D. 1613, and was made an independent Raja for assassinating, by order of Prince Khoorm, son of Jahangir by a princess of Amber, Govind Das, a faithful Rajput. This was done to disgust the Rahtores, and it drove Raja Guj Singh away from the court at Delhi. Prince Khoorm next had his elder brother Parvéz assassinated, and proceeded to the deposition of his father, who rallied the Rajput princes to his aid.

AMRA SINGH. P. 63

"In the month of Bysak, S. 1690 (A.D. 1634), five years before the death of Raja Guj, in a convocation of all the feudality of Maroo, sentence of exclusion from the succession was pronounced upon Umra, accompanied by the solemn and seldom-practised rite of *Dés-vatoh* or exile. This ceremony, which is marked as a day of mourning in the calendar, was attended with all the circumstances of funeral pomp. As soon as the sentence was pronounced, that his birthright was forfeited and assigned to his junior brother, and that he ceased to be a subject of Maroo, the *khilat* of banishment was brought forth, consisting of sable vestments, in which he was clad; a sable shield was hung upon his back, and a sword of the same hue girded round him; a black horse was then led out, being mounted on which, he was commanded, though not in anger, to depart whither he listed beyond the limits of Maroo."—Tod's *Annals of Marwar.*

"*BUT ARUNG THRUST HIS ISLAM DOWN OUR THROATS.*" P. 71

"In such detestation did the Hindus hold this intolerant king, that in like manner as they supposed the beneficent Akber to be the devout Mokund in a former birth, so they make the tyrant's body enclose the soul of Kal-Yamun, the foe of Crishna, ere his apotheosis, from whom he fled to Dwarica, and thence acquired the name of Rinchor.

"Rin, the 'field of battle'—chor, from chorna, 'to abandon.'"—Tod, vol. i. p. 523.

In his poem of *Akbar's Dream* Tennyson represents the liberality of Akbar's creed and the intolerance of Aurangzeb's.

"I hate the rancour of their castes and creeds,
I let men worship as they will, I reap
No revenue from the field of unbelief.
I cull from every faith and race the best
And bravest soul for counsellor and friend.
I loathe the very name of infidel.
I stagger at the Koran and the sword.
I shudder at the Christian and the stake."

In his vision after death Akbar says—

"I watched my son,
And those that followed, loosen, stone from stone,
All my fair work; and from the ruin arose
The shriek and curse of trampled millions, even
As in the time before; but while I groaned,
From out the sunset poured an alien race,
Who fitted stone to stone again, and Truth,
Peace, Love and Justice came and dwelt therein;
Nor in the field without were seen or heard
Fires of suttee, nor wail of baby-wife,
Or Indian widow; and in sleep I said,
'All praise to Alla by whatever hands
My mission be accomplished!'"

FOUNDING OF BIKANIR. P. 75

"It is seldom that so incontestable a title to supremacy can be asserted as that which the weakness and jealousies of the Godarras conferred upon Beeka; and it is a pleasing incident to find almost throughout India, in the observance of certain rites, the remembrance of the original compact which transferred the sovereign power from the lords of the soil to their Rajpoot conquerors. Thus in Méwar the fact of the power conferred upon the Ghelote founder by the Bhil aborigines is commemorated by a custom brought down to the present times. At Ambér the same is recorded in the important offices retained by the Meenas, the primitive inhabitants of that land. Both Kotah and Boondi retain in their names the remembrance of the ancient lords of Harouti; and Beeka's descendants preserve, in a twofold manner, the recollection of their bloodless conquest of the Jits. To this day the descendant of Pandú applies the unguent of royalty to the forehead of the successors of Beeka; on which occasion the prince places 'the fine of relief,' consisting of twenty-five pieces of gold, in the hand of the Jit. Moreover, the spot which he selected for his capital was the birthright of a Jit, who would only concede it for this purpose on the condition that his name should be linked in perpetuity with its surrender. Naira, or Néra, was the name of the proprietor, which Beeka added to his own, thus composing that of the future capital, Bíkanér."—Tod's *Annals of Bikaner.*

ANECDOTE OF PUNCTILIO RELATED IN POWLETT'S "GAZETTEER OF BIKANIR." P. 83

"In Sambat 1870 (A.D. 1813) the two chiefs of Bikanir and Jodhpur became friends, a Guru, Aishji by name, having acted as peacemaker between them. Surat Singh agreed to meet Man Singh at Nagor, and on his way visited Karniji's temple, walking on foot through the surrounding wood. At Nagore a difficulty occurred, owing to Man Singh's objecting to meet Surat Singh on terms of perfect equality. At length Aishji overcame the difficulty by arranging that the Maharajas should neither of them sit on a cushion, which was to be occupied by the Guru alone, while the chiefs sat on

a carpet. Another sacred character having to occupy a seat lower than the Maharaja vindicated his dignity by tying up his head during the durbar. The Guru exhorted the chiefs to brotherly kindness and caused them to eat together."

RAJA GAJ SINGH OF BIKANIR AND RAJA BIJEY SINGH OF JODHPORE. P. 91

Gaj Singh was Raja of Bikanir from 1745 A.D. to 1788 A.D. He successfully resisted an invasion upon Bikanir territory from Jodhpur under Raja Abhai Singh, and helped Bakht Singh to defeat his brother Abhai Singh and oust him from the Gadi (A.D. 1751). On the death of Bakht Singh his son Bijai Singh received great assistance from Gaj Singh in various fights besides the incident referred to in the Rhyme.[1] Allied by marriage with Jesalmere and on friendly terms with Jeypore, Jodhpore, and Mewar, Gaj Singh exalted the Bikanir raj considerably. Once after consulting Karniji, a Charan woman worshipped as an incarnation of Devi, and the patron saint of Bikanir, he accompanied Bijai Singh of Jodhpur to Nathdwara, the famous temple of Sri Krishn, and is said to have astonished even the Gosain there by his learning. The Maharana of Mewar begged him to mediate between him and Jodhpur for the restoration of Godwar which had been entrusted to the latter by Mewar for merely temporary custody, but in this he was unsuccessful.

Powlett in his *Gazetteer for Bikanir* writes as follows on this point (p. 62):—

[1] Tod gives quite a different version of this story. He attributes the saving of the Raja to one of the Jeypore nobles who sat on the skirt of the Maharaja's robe and prevented his rising, and he does not mention the Raja of Bikanir or his two Thakurs.

"The Rana begged Gaj Singh to help him to arrange his difficulties with his nobles and Bijai Singh. Gaj Singh did his best to get Bijai to act in concert with him, but Bijai did not wish the anarchy which then prevailed in Mewar to cease, as it strengthened his hold on Godwar, and both the Rana and the Kishengurh chief told Gaj Singh that it was useless his incurring further trouble and expense by remaining at Nathdwara in hopes of prevailing with the Jodhpur chief. Gaj Singh was convinced of the truth of this, but he resolved on a last effort to induce Bijai Singh to give up Godwar, and with that object he arranged to visit the temple with him, where the Rana by previous agreement also came. Gaj Singh on meeting Bijai in the presence of the Rana again urged him to restore Godwar, and when he failed the Gosain of the temple told Bijai that it was the command of the deity that he should comply. The Jodhpur chief thus pressed turned to his followers and said, 'Well, the Rana must have your pergunna,' whereupon Zorawur Singh of Kiūsar, always forward, and perhaps perceiving that his master wanted support, exclaimed: 'Hear, ye nobles of Marwar, Godwar is not Bijai Singh's to give: he is indeed lord of the Rahtors but not of the land: that you must get from us, and we will die before we part with it, and you will die before you get it.' This speech settled the matter and the chiefs parted."

BIJEY SINGH ON HIS DEATH-BED. P. 101

Bijey Singh's ill-luck was proverbial, though his personal gallantry was never doubted. Tod quotes a native bard as saying—"Fortune never attended the stirrup of Bijey Singh, who never gained a battle though at the head of a hundred thousand men; but Ram Singh (his cousin and rival) by his valour and conduct gained victories by the handful."

The following extract from a subsequent page of the same historian shows that Bijey Singh's misfortunes in the field were not due to him personally, though at the end of his reign, which lasted thirty-one years, the license of his morals even in that loose age and an imbecile attachment to a woman helped to estrange his nobles and complete the anarchy of the country.

"Marwar had enjoyed several years of peace, when the rapid strides made by the Mahrattas towards universal rapine, if not conquest, compelled the Rajpoots once more to form an union for the defence of their political existence. Pertáp Sing, a prince of energy and enterprise, was now on the gadi of Ambér. In S. 1843 (A.D. 1787) he sent an ambassador to Beejy Sing, proposing a league against the common foe, and volunteering to lead in person their conjoined forces against them. The battle of Tonga ensued, in which Rahtore valour shone forth in all its glory. Despising discipline, they charged through the dense battalions of De Boigne, sabring his artillery-men at their guns, and compelling Sindia to abandon not only the field, but all his conquests for a time. Beejy Sing, by this victory, redeemed the castle of Ajmér, and declared his tributary alliance null and void. But the genius of Sindia, and the talents of De Boigne, soon recovered this loss; and in four years the Mahratta marched with a force such as Indian warfare was stranger to, to redeem that day's disgrace. In S. 1847 (A.D. 1791) the murderous battles of Patun and Mairta took place, in which Rajpoot courage was heroically but fruitlessly displayed against European tactics and unlimited resources, and where neither intrigue nor treason was wanting. The result was the imposition of a contribution of sixty lacs of rupees, or £600,000; and as so much could not be drained from the country, goods and chattels were everywhere distrained, and hostages given for the balance.

"Ajmér, which had revolted on the short-lived triumph of Tonga, was once more surrendered, and lost for ever to Marwar. When invested by De Boigne, the faithful governor, Dumraj, placed in the dilemma of a disgraceful surrender or disobedience to his prince's summons, swallowed diamond-powder. 'Tell the raja,' said this faithful servant, 'thus only could I testify my obedience; and over my dead body alone could a Southron enter Ajmér.'"—Tod, vol. ii. pp. 133-134.

JESALMERE. P. 104

"The majority of the inhabitants of Jaisalmer State are Yadu Bhati Rajputs and claim a very ancient lineage. They take their name from an ancestor named Bhati, who was renowned as a warrior when the tribe were settled in the Punjab. The clan was driven southwards by the King of Ghazni across the Sutlej and found a refuge in the Indian Desert, which has been henceforth their home. It is probable, according to Tod, that, like the Rahtore Rajputs, the clan is descended from one of the Indo-Scythic tribes, who penetrated into Hindustan at a very remote period. The Bhatis, subsequent to their entry into the desert tract, engaged in constant struggles with the neighbouring tribes, whom they overcame. They established themselves successively at Tarnot, Deoráwal, and Jaisalmer. Deoráwal was founded by Deoraj, who is esteemed the real founder of the present ruling family. Deoraj was the first to take the title of Ráwal. He is said to have been born in 836 A.D. In 1156 Jaisal, the sixth in succession from Deoraj, founded the fort and city of Jaisalmer, and made it his capital. Jaisal was succeeded by several warlike princes, who were constantly engaged in raids and battles. But the taste for freebooting proved disastrous. On two occasions, namely in 1294 and shortly afterwards, the Bhatis so enraged the Emperor Alá-ud-din that the imperial army captured and sacked the fort and city of Jaisalmer, which for some time remained deserted. The reign of Ráwal Sabal Singh marks an epoch in Bhati history, for this prince, by acknowledging the supremacy of Sháh Jahán, was the first of his line to hold his dominions as a fief of the Delhi Empire.

Jaisalmer had now arrived at the height of its power; the territory extended north to the Sutlej, comprised the whole of Baháwalpur westward to the Indus, and to the east and south included many districts subsequently annexed by the Rahtores, and incorporated in Jodhpur and Bikaner. But from this time till the accession of Ráwal Mulráj in 1762 the fortunes of the State rapidly declined, and most of the outlying provinces were wrested from Jaisalmer. Owing, however, to its isolated situation, the State escaped the ravages of the Marathas." (*Imperial Gazetteer of India.*)

According to Tod, the local bards say that when Jesalmere was stormed and captured by Nawab Mahboob Khan in A.D. 1295 it had been besieged for nine years. 16,000 Musalmans and all the garrison, with 24,000 females immolated at the Johur, are said to have perished. The Mahomedans kept the castle for two years and then abandoned the place. A few years after Dudha repaired Jesalmere and raided on Ajmere. This led to a second assault by the Mahomedans. For services rendered to Timoor Shah the chief Gursi obtained a grant of his hereditary domains and re-established Jesalmere A.D. 1306.

INFANTICIDE. P. 112

"The Dahima emptied his coffers" (says Chund, the pole-star of the Rajpoots) "on the marriage of his daughter with Pirthiraj; but he filled them 'with the praises of mankind.' The same bard retails every article of these daejas or 'dowers,' which thus become precedents for future ages; and the 'lac passao' then established for the chief bardai has become a model to posterity. Even now the Rana of Oodipoor, in his season of poverty, at the recent marriage of his daughter bestowed 'the gift of a lac' on the chief bard; though the articles of gold, horses, clothes, etc., were included in the estimate, and at an undue valuation, which rendered the gift not quite so precious as in the days of the Chohan."—Tod, vol. i. p. 638.

RANTHAMBOR. P. 122

"From the time of its surrender by Rao Soorjun to Akber, the importance of this castle was established by its becoming the first *sircar*, or 'department,' in the province of Ajmér, consisting of no less than 'eighty-three mahals,' or extensive fiefs, in which were comprehended not only Boondi and Kotah, and all their dependencies, but the entire state of Scopoor, and all the petty fiefs south of the Bangunga, the aggregate of which now constitutes the state of Ambér. In fact, with the exception of Mahmoodabad in Bengal, Rinthumbor was the most extensive sircar of the empire. In the decrepitude of the empire, this castle was maintained by a veteran commander as long as funds and provisions lasted; but these failing, in order to secure it from falling into the hands of the Mahrattas, and thus being lost for ever to the throne, he sought out a Rajpoot prince, to whom he might entrust it. He applied to Boondi; but the Hara, dreading to compromise his fealty if unable to maintain it, refused the boon, and having no alternative, he resigned it to the prince of Ambér as a trust which he could no longer defend."—Tod, vol. ii. pp. 492-493.

THE DISCROWNING OF UMÉD SINGH. P. 123

In his *Annals of Haraoti* (chapter iv.) Tod tells how the young Omeda fought against the Jeypore army.

"The steed of Oméda was struck by a cannon-ball, and the intestines protruded from the wound. The intrepidity of the youthful hero, nobly seconded by his kin and clan, was unavailing; and the chieftains, fearing he would throw away a life the preservation of which they all desired, entreated he would abandon the contest; observing 'that if he survived, Boondi must be theirs; but if he was slain, there was an end of all their hopes.'

"With grief he submitted; and as they gained the Sowalli Pass, which leads to Indurgurh, he dismounted to breathe his faithful steed; and as he loosened the girths, it expired. Oméda sat down and wept. Hunja was worthy of such a mark of his esteem: he was a steed of Irâk, the gift of the king to his father, whom he had borne in many an encounter. Nor was this natural ebullition of the young Hara a transient feeling: Hunja's memory was held in veneration, and the first act of Oméda, when he recovered his throne, was to erect a statue to the steed who bore him so nobly on the day of Dublana. It stands in the square (*chouk*) of the city, and receives the reverence of each Hara, who links his history with one of the brightest of their achievements, though obscured by momentary defeat.

"Oméda gained Indurgurh, which was close at hand, on foot; but this traitor to the name of Hara, who had acknowledged the supremacy of Ambér, not only refused his prince a horse in his adversity, but warned him off the domain, asking 'if he meant to be the ruin of Indurgurh as well as Boondi?' Disdaining to drink water within its bounds, the young prince, stung by this perfidious mark of inhospitality, took the direction of Kurwain.

Its chief made amends for the other's churlishness: he advanced to meet him, offered such aid as he had to give, and presented him with a horse. Dismissing his faithful kinsmen to their homes, and begging their swords when fortune might be kinder, he regained his old retreat, the ruined palace of Rampoora, amongst the ravines of the Chumbul."

Tod adds the following foot-note :—

"I have made my salaam to the representative of Hunja, and should have graced his neck with a chaplet on every military festival, had I dwelt among the Haras."

The act which led to the abdication of Uméd Singh after he had recovered his dominions is thus related :—

"An act of revenge stained the reputation of Oméda, naturally virtuous, and but for which deed we should have to paint him as one of the bravest, wisest, and most faultless characters which Rajpoot history has recorded. Eight years had elapsed since the recovery of his dominions, and we have a right to infer that his wrongs and their authors had been forgotten, or rather forgiven, for human nature can scarcely forget so treacherous an act as that of his vassal of Indurgurh, on the defeat of Dublana. As so long a time had passed since the restoration without the penalty of his treason being exacted, it might have been concluded that the natural generosity of this high-minded prince had co-operated with a wise policy, in passing over the wrong without foregoing his right to avenge it. The degenerate Rajpoot, who could at such a moment witness the necessities of his prince and refuse to relieve them, could never reflect on that hour without self-abhorrence; but his spirit was too base to offer reparation by a future life of duty; he cursed the magnanimity of the man he had injured, hated him for his very forbearance, and aggravated the part he had acted by fresh injuries, and on a point too delicate to admit of being overlooked. Oméda had 'sent the coco-nut,' the symbol of matrimonial alliance, to Madhu Sing, in the name of his sister. It was received in a full assembly of all the nobles of the court, and with the respect due to one of the most illustrious races of Rajpootana. Deo Sing of Indurgurh was at that time on a visit at Jeipoor, and the compliment was paid him by the Raja of asking 'what fame said of the daughter of Boodh Sing?' It is not impossible that he might have sought this opportunity of further betraying his prince: for his reply was an insulting innuendo, leading to doubts as to the purity of her blood. That it was grossly false was soon proved by the solicitation of her hand by Raja Beejy Sing of Marwar. The coco-nut was returned to Boondi—an insult never to be forgiven by a Rajpoot.

"In S. 1813 (A.D. 1757) Oméda went to pay his devotions at the shrine of Beejaséni Máta ('the mother of victory'), near Kurwur. Being in the vicinity of Indurgurh, he invited its chief to join the assembled vassals with their families; and though dissuaded, Deo Sing obeyed, accompanied by his son and grandson. All were cut off at one fell swoop, and the line of the traitor was extinct: as if the air of heaven should not be contaminated by the smoke of their ashes, Oméda commanded that the body of the calumnious traitor and his issue should be thrown into the lake. His fief of Indurgurh was given to his brother, between whom and the present incumbent four generations have passed away.

"Fifteen years elapsed, during which the continual scenes of disorder around him furnished ample occupation for his thoughts. Yet, in the midst of all, would intrude the remembrance of this single act, in which he had usurped the powers of Him to whom alone it belongs to execute vengeance. Though no voice was lifted up against the deed, though he had a moral conviction that a traitor's death was the due of Deo Sing, his soul, generous as it was brave, revolted at the crime, however sanctified by custom,[1] which confounds the innocent with the guilty. To appease his conscience, he determined to abdicate the throne and pass the rest of his days in penitential rites, and traversing, in the pilgrim's garb, the vast regions of India, to visit the sacred shrines of his faith.

"In S. 1827 (A.D. 1771) the imposing ceremony of 'joograj,' which terminated the political existence of Oméda, was performed. An image of the prince was made, and a pyre was erected, on which it was consumed. The hair and whiskers of Ajit, his successor, were taken off, and offered to the manes; lamentation and wailing were heard in the rinwâs,[2] and the twelve days of matum, or 'mourning,' were passed as if Oméda had really deceased; on the expiration of which, the installation of his successor took place, when Ajit Sing was proclaimed prince of the Haras of Boondi."—Tod, vol. ii. pp. 494-495.

THE JATS. P. 140

In his *History of the Rajput Tribes* Tod writes:—"In all the ancient catalogues of the thirty-six royal races of India the Jit has a place, though by none is he ever styled 'Rajpoot'; nor am I aware of any instance of a Rajpoot's intermarriage with a Jit. It is a name widely disseminated over

---

[1] "The laws of revenge are dreadfully absolute: had the sons of Deo Sing survived, the feud upon their liege lord would have been entailed with their estate. It is a nice point for a subject to balance between fidelity to his prince and a father's feud."

[2] The queen's apartments.

India, though it does not now occupy a very elevated place amongst the inhabitants, belonging chiefly to the agricultural classes.

"In the Punjab they still retain their ancient name of Jit. On the Jumna and Ganges they are styled Jats, of whom the chief of Bhurtpoor is the most conspicuous. On the Indus and on Saurashtra they are termed Juts. The greater portion of the husbandmen in Rajast'han are Jits; and there are numerous tribes beyond the Indus, now proselytes to the Mahomedan religion, who derive their origin from this class."

Sir Lepel Griffin in his recent book on Ranjit Singh (*Rulers of India* series) writes:—

"The origin of the Jats is shrouded in much uncertainty and has been the subject of long discussion. Some distinguished writers have found for them a Getic origin, but the traditions of the Punjab Jats in almost all cases refer to a Rajput descent, and emigration to the Punjab from Central India."

* * * * *

"They hold a social place below the Brahman, the Rajput, and the Khattri, but they themselves assert an equality with the second and a superiority over the third of these castes, a claim which their historical record and present importance justify. They are seen at their best in the Sikh districts above the rivers Beas and Sutlej."

* * * * * *

"The virtues of the Jats are thus identical with those of the Sikhs who have come out of this caste."

"*NOT ONE WHITE SOLDIER NEAR.*" Pp. 143, 144

In his narrative of events in Rajputana during the Mutiny the Governor-General's Agent, Brigadier-General G. St. P. Lawrence, wrote :—

"There was not a single European soldier in Rajpootana"; and in a later paragraph thus described the loyal attitude of the Rajput princes and people generally during the Mutiny :—

"I would point out that with three distinct mutinies in its heart, with every element for both Moslem and Hindoo fanaticism, with a dangerous combination among Marwar and other malcontent nobles, with a rebel nucleus at Mundisore close to its southern frontier, with thousands of discarded Hindoos of the lowest class in the ranks of the armies of its princes in Rajpootana, the revolt in India was met with *no* sympathy from Rajpoot rulers, nobles, or population generally; that whilst our provinces have been disorganised scenes of riot and slaughter, this vast territory has hardly called for any armed interference, but has remained a rock of strength, and blessed the wise and just policy which has made the British power, relieving that of the Tartar and Mahratta dynasty, so respected and welcome, as to make the Rajpoot feel his interests identical with ours, and his independent freedom in the scale with the maintenance of British supremacy."

ULWAR. P. 145

We hear of Mewat, the country which now comprises more than half the Ulwar State, doing homage to Bisaldeo Chauhan of Ajmere in A.D. 764. It appears then to have belonged to Jadu Rajputs. In A.D. 1235 it was apparently under the control of Emperor Shamsuddin Altamash, and the

Mewattis generally had accepted the faith, with Hindu observances still grafted on to it, of their Mahomedan conquerors. The famous Bahadur Nahar, the reputed founder of the Khanzadas, was originally a Jadu Rajput, and the Mewatti chief Hasun Khan assisted the Rajputs in resisting Babar who subjugated the country in A.D. 1526.

Aurangzeb gave Ulwar in jagir to Sawai Jai Singh of Jeypore who held it for a few years. The Jats from Bhurtpore overran the country from A.D. 1720 to about 1770, when the Narukas, a sept descended from the Kachwahas of Jeypore, joined in the struggle, and their first chief Partap Singh held the fort and town from 1775 to 1791, when he was succeeded by Bukhtawar Singh who ruled till 1815. Then the third chief Banni Singh, who is held in high estimation by his people, ruled till 1857, when he was succeeded by Sheodan Singh who died in 1874, being succeeded by Mungal Singh.

THE END

Printed by R. & R. CLARK, *Edinburgh.*

